Literacy Shutdown

Stories of Six American Women

Literacy Shutdown

Stories of Six American Women

Daphne Key

INTERNATIONAL **Reading** **Association**

800 Barksdale Road
PO Box 8139
Newark, Delaware 19714-8139, USA
www.reading.org

nrc
NATIONAL READING CONFERENCE

National Reading Conference
122 South Michigan Avenue
Suite 1100
llinois 60603, USA

Director of Publications   Joan M. Irwin
Assistant Director of Publications   Jeanette K. Moss
Editor-in-Chief, Books   Christian A. Kempers
Senior Editor   Matthew W. Baker
Assistant Editor   Janet S. Parrack
Assistant Editor   Mara P. Gorman
Publications Coordinator   Beth Doughty
Association Editor   David K. Roberts
Production Department Manager   Iona Sauscermen
Art Director   Boni Nash
Electronic Publishing Supervisor   Wendy A. Mazur
Electronic Publishing Specialist   Anette Schütz-Ruff
Electronic Publishing Specialist   Cheryl J. Strum
Electronic Publishing Assistant   Peggy Mason

Library of Congress Cataloging in Publication Data
    Key, Daphne.
    Literacy shutdown : Stories of six American women / Daphne Key.
        p.   cm.—(Literacy studies series)
    Includes bibliographical references and index.
    1. Women—Education—Southern States—Case studies.   2. Literacy—Social aspects—
Southern States—Case studies.   3. Women—Southern States—Social conditions—Case stud-
ies.   I. International Reading Association.   II. National Reading Conference (U.S.)   III. Title.
IV. Series.
LC1752.K49   1998   98-34002
302.2'244—dc21
ISBN 0-87207-196-0

Contents

Note From The Series Editors

In an era when explorations of the universe are commonplace, and when we have made such giant strides in tolerance among people, why is literacy shutdown an issue for many students?

Through the voices of women who have experienced literacy shutdown, Daphne Key's book *Literacy Shutdown: Stories of Six American Women*, the third in the Literacy Studies Series, offers insights about the causes of this literacy dysfunction. We believe that the stories of these women will aid us in our mission to eradicate illiteracy and aliteracy.

We hope this volume plays the important role of informing teachers, researchers, and the larger educational community about the issues that cause, affect, and reverse literacy shutdown. We further hope that this excellent volume will serve as a reference tool as educators plan literacy programs for learners of all ages and cultures. This book as well as others in the Literacy Studies Series broadens our understanding of research and provides guidance as instructional practices are designed. The goal of the series is to advance knowledge in the field of literacy and to help make research a more important focus in the literacy community. The volumes in the series are intended to inform literacy instruction and research by reporting findings from state-of-the-art literacy endeavors. We believe that this text successfully accomplishes this goal.

James Flood
Diane Lapp
Series Editors
San Diego State University
San Diego, California, USA

Review Board

Dr. Jennifer Battle
Southwest Texas State University
San Marcos, Texas

Dr. Cynthia Brock
Texas Womenís University
Denton, Texas

Dr. Victoria Chou
University of Illinois at Chicago
Chicago, Illinois

Dr. Karin L. Dahl
Ohio State University
Columbus, Ohio

Dr. Douglas Fisher
San Diego State University
San Diego, California

Dr. James Flood (series co-editor)
San Diego State University
San Diego, California

Dr. Margie Gallego
University of California at
   San Diego
LaJolla, California

Dr. Susan Mandel Glazer
Ryder University
Lawrenceville, New Jersey

Dr. Dana Grisham
San Diego State University
San Diego, California

Dr. Diane Lapp (series co-editor)
San Diego State University
San Diego, California

Dr. Miriam Martinez
University of Texas–San Antonio
San Antonio, Texas

Dr. Lesley Mandel Morrow
Rutgers University
New Brunswick, New Jersey

Dr. Nancy Nelson
Louisiana State University
Baton Rouge, Louisiana

Dr. Susan B. Neuman
Temple University
Philadelphia, Pennsylvania

Dr. Nancy C. Padak
Kent State University
Kent, Ohio

Dr. Jeanne R. Paratore
Boston University
Boston, Massachusetts

Dr. Victoria Purcell-Gates
Harvard University
Cambridge, Massachusetts

Dr. Nancy L. Roser
University of Texas
Austin, Texas

Dr. Diane L. Schallert
University of Texas
Austin, Texas

Dr. Lyndon W. Searfoss
Arizona State University
Tucson, Arizona

Dr. Peter N. Winograd
University of New Mexico
Albuquerque, New Mexico

Dr. M. Jo Worthy
University of Texas at Austin
Austin, Texas

Foreword

Prevailing attitudes toward literacy in any era or province implicitly point to the values of that culture. *Literacy Shutdown* seems no less prophetic and challenging than did James Baldwin's *The Fire Next Time* (1963). As did Baldwin's treatise, *Literacy Shutdown* inspires, challenges, exhorts through the evocation of possibilities, and warns of the perils attending the neglect of phenomena directly related to the well being of the populace.

This work is both a social commentary and a scholarly critique, dramatizing the interrelationship between literacy and the human spirit. Literacy as a set of skills achieved according to some kind of cognitive hierarchy or paradigm is a reductive concept in relation to the purposes of this book. Literacy here is given more latitude as a concept with appropriate recognition of the complex dynamic it really is.

Perhaps no one book could end, definitively, the ageless pedagogical debate about the appropriate distribution of academic rigor and concern for the human spirit. However, this book may alter the character and depth of that debate. Neither proponents of rigor at all costs nor apologists for compromising excellence for the survival of the human spirit will find solace here. Rather they will find the continuing challenge of measuring and understanding literacy as defined in this work: "reading and writing and what these acts make possible."

The part of that definition—"what these acts make possible"—is pivotal for a clear understanding of silencing, distancing, and non-reciprocity. The experiences of the six American women chronicled here expand the meaning of these terms, making them much more than abstractions. We listen to the voices of these women who can recall with frightening specificity the day and the act precipitating their own literacy shutdown. No person in a position of power can consider both the impact and permanence of these negations without assuming some measure of guilt or obligation to intervene.

Not one woman described in the volume seemed to consider excellence or "correctness" to be unreasonable, but they all voiced the sense of uneasiness and insufficiency they experienced in the presence of this criteria. None could completely put to rest the wounds, the fears, or the uncertainties attending their own communicative shutdown. And they dramatize convincingly the futility of attempting to separate human communication from self-worth, comfort, and other positive states theoretically of concern to the academy and society in general. We witness here their pleading through the author for higher praise than a shrug, the embarrassment evoked by a public correction of a grammatical fault, and the expectation of failure they intuit from what they perceive to be a class-conscious teacher—all contributing to literacy shutdown.

Having one's language criticized is tantamount to personal rejection. Key illustrates in this work the relationship between acceptance of a person's language and acceptance of the person. Her work creates a challenge for scholars, who as human beings interact with others and attach value to the use of language and the nature of the reception it receives in important personal and social transactions.

The author brings both passion and sophistication to the issue of literacy, along with a willingness to challenge her own arrogance in relation to literacy. The distance between the communicative ease of the educated often translates not into an overt bearing of superiority but into a subtle yet insidious lowering of sensitivity to the real and intense insecurity among those with lesser fluency. I predict that these stories will begin to bridge that gap, making each constituency braver and more willing to meet in the middle, thus obviating the unnecessary fear and guilt accompanying literacy shutdown. I see *Literacy Shutdown* as a work for the 21st century—providing insight into an intricate phenomenon that will, no doubt, evoke interest and encourage debate at many levels of polity for years to come.

Robbie Jean Walker
Auburn University
Montgomery, Alabama, USA

Acknowledgments

I am indebted to all who have taught me about language and literacy —the research participants, the child-care providers in Alabama, my students, my father and mother, and my special teachers and mentors: Sophia Mayo, Guy Owen, Richard Graves, Frank Walters, and Terry Ley. I am indebted also to those whom I have never met but who have enlightened me through their own writing—their own use of literacy to good purpose: Deborah Brandt, Linda Brodkey, Paulo Freire, Anne Ruggles Gere, Shirley Brice Heath, Mike Rose, Mina Shaughnessy, and Kurt Spellmeyer. I am thankful they never shut down or feared voicing their opinions. I thank James Flood and Diane Lapp for their faith and their invitation to enter a new world of possibility. I thank Janet Parrack for her incredible patience and her willingness to help a beginning writer, for I often fought my own insecurities, my own desire to shut down. I thank Robbie Walker for her help and wisdom. To my dear friends, Carol Shaw and Tony Shaw, I appreciate your help at a critical time in the creation of this book. But especially, to my husband, Larry, and my daughter, Jane, I am thankful that they encouraged me to keep writing.

Language, Literacy, and Arrogance: An Introduction

For months, I spent many hours with six women—African American and white—from different life circumstances in the United States. We sat at their kitchen tables, and they shared their language and literacy experiences. When I questioned these literate women, I focused on their "shutting down" in relation to language and literacy use. Their stories recounted here reveal their reluctance to read, to write, and to speak publicly, and their feelings for this need to shut down in the presence of others deemed more powerful, more correct, or more educated. Their stories also capture moments when some of them resisted shutting down and bravely dared to reveal and use their language and literacy skills in front of others.

What has been perceived as illiteracy or a failure to master reading and writing skills may be, in many cases, failure to resist shutting down in response to those in positions of power. Powerful people may consciously or subconsciously desire to distance themselves from those whose backgrounds—which include their literacy capital and linguistic repertoire—may differ from their own. Those in power therefore often drive others to silence as they shut them out of their worlds.[1]

Many teachers now recognize that literacy and language are not decontextualized; rather, in the words of Deborah Brandt (1990), they understand more about the nature of literacy as a "metacognitive ability—an increasing awareness of and control over the social means by which people sustain discourse, knowledge, and reality" (p. 32). They recognize that literacy and language are inextricably bound to economic and political systems and to a sense of family and community. However, *literacy* and *language* can be used as indicators to judge another person, because in the United States, as well as in other countries, one's manner of speech and one's literacy capital reflect one's status in the community. James C. Raymond (1982) commented, "People who are highly literate, like people who are very rich, are tempted to regard literacy or money as the measure of human worth" (p. 12). Teachers and those in power in the United States usually possess the preferred linguistic capital—they are highly literate. Unfortunately, those who measure human worth by one's possessions or status are often arrogant, perhaps unintentionally, believing that their manner of speaking and their education are superior. This arrogance about language and literacy permeates human encounters and influences self-worth and attitudes about the purposes of literacy in everyday living. Raymond stated that Mina Shaughnessy's *Errors and Expectations* (1977) highlighted a necessary perspective on literacy—one often overlooked in academic debates about cognitive psychology, linguistics, whole language, phonics, standard English, and testing—that is our ability "to perceive the human value" of people in relation to their language and their literacy capital (p. 15). It is this perspective on which I wish to focus.

I have spent most of my teaching career working with students who were in some way marginalized. I have observed students who knew that they did not possess the appropriate linguistic or cultural capital necessary for acceptance when reading, writing, or speaking in front of others who spoke correctly and were better educated. I have seen hurt, rebuke, fear, defensiveness, and withdrawal on their faces, and I have seen them shut down and refuse to use literacy even though they could read, write, and speak. I taught composition and reading at a community college near Washington, D.C., where the diversity of the student population reflects the changing racial and ethnic make-up of schools across the United States. Most of my students were not middle-class white students; rather, they were from Algeria, Bolivia, Ecuador, El Salvador, Ethiopia, France, India, Iran, Japan, Korea, Nigeria, Paraguay, and Vietnam. Although this level of racial and ethnic diversity may not be present everywhere in the United States, Catherine Walsh (1991) stated that "approximately one third of the

2

U.S. school population are students of color" and approximately "three million of these are students for whom English is a second language, a majority of whom are of Latino background" (p. 3). In the literacy narratives[2] I assign my students, they describe their experiences with language and literacy in U.S. schools. They frequently tell me that they decided to shut down rather than face ridicule and failure when speaking, reading, or writing in school. I spend a great deal of time attempting to restore their confidence, and their sense of human value.

A wide range of literature suggests that I am not alone in dealing with students whose linguistic repertoires do not match the standards of English usage handbooks. The experiences of marginalized students who shut down in relation to literacy use and the experiences of those in power who inadvertently shut them out of literacy encounters also are reflected in the research and writing of Linda Brodkey (1990), Ellen Cushman (1996), Karin Dahl and Penny Freppon (1995), Nan Elsasser and Patricia Irvine (1992), Michelle Fine (1992), Anne Ruggles Gere (1994), Shirley Brice Heath (1983), William Labov (1972), John Ogbu (1987, 1991, 1994), Kathleen Rockhill (1993), Mike Rose (1990), and Denny Taylor (1983). Although there are many others, I list these scholars and researchers because their work has informed my own. Their areas of expertise and theoretical stances are varied, and the subjects of their research represent the United States's diversity: inner-city elementary school children, high school students, and adults from various social classes and racial and ethnic groups. In the work of both Rose and Fine, the term "shut down" emerges. Yet in reading the work of these researchers, I sensed Maria Lugones's (1987) concept of "arrogant perception" influencing literacy and language use as it related to people's perceptions of their own human value and their need to shut down. I believe that the concept of arrogant perception is universal and worthy of contemplation in relation to language and literacy use.

My own research on which this book is based occurred because seven African American women in Alabama gave me a plaque. About 10 years ago, I stopped teaching English. I could not fail one more developmental writing student who could not master standard English conventions in one semester. I took a job in a nonprofit agency in Montgomery, Alabama, which had won a grant, and I began a community literacy project. In this project I saw women, some of whom had not graduated from high school, who were reading and writing to produce stories for children in their day-care centers. They admitted that they had often felt intimidated reading and writing in school in front of "correct" teachers. The women in this literacy project stayed together for a year until the grant money ran out, but during the year they established libraries in their day-care centers, performed in plays, and held storytelling events in several counties. In this project they refused to shut down or to be shut out of these literacy events; they decided to use the literacy skills they had and not fear correction by me or anyone else. After this experience, I could not go back into an English classroom until I determined why these women, some of whom had shut down in school, had not done so in this literacy project. All of them could read and write beautifully. On the plaque they presented me were haunting, engraved words for me to ponder. They thanked me for "sacrificing enough to allow others to grow." What had I sacrificed in this community literacy project that I had not sacrificed in my English classes?

I turned to graduate school to find answers. One evening at Auburn University (Alabama) in Dr. Richard Graves's class, a discussion about language usage ignited suddenly. The room became polarized. Some veteran teachers and graduate students, in frustration and anger, declared their mission to correct incorrect and substandard usage. Another group, equally emotional, demanded tolerance. I went home and wrote all night. That memorable class discussion and my own writing that night revealed to me that the real or the perceived arrogance of persons in power is linked inextricably to the willingness to read, write, or speak of those not in power, a willingness that often has no correlation to their ability to read, write, or speak. I finally understood that arrogance can impede literacy's potential and that arrogant perceptions about race, class, and literacy and linguistic background must be sacrificed. I had never thought of myself as an arrogant person. However, I wondered if it was arrogance that I in some way had sacrificed in the literacy project in Montgomery.

In my research, I explored women's recollections of communicative shutdown and literacy success as aspects of literacy practices based on Brian Street's (1993) definition: "'Literacy practices' incor-

4

porate not only 'literacy events', as empirical occasions to which literacy is integral, but also as 'folk models' of those events and the ideological preconceptions that underpin them" (pp. 12–13). In the women's stories I recount, these practices are moments in daily life when reading, writing, and speaking are critical—a moment, for example, when a person must have a letter of reference for a job or when a passionately written essay wins a young woman college admission after her guidance counselor told her she is not college material. Their recollections of literacy practices are tied intricately to class, gender, and racial and geographic perceptions of identity; they are not decontextualized.

The women described in this book recalled moments when they had chosen not to read, write, or speak for fear of ridicule, embarrassment, or manipulation. Instead, they retreated into silence. Some avoided jobs requiring writing; some avoided furthering their education. Being perceived as "incorrect"—and having one's incorrectness confirmed by possible spelling, usage, reading, or speech errors—was not worth the risk. Many of the women shut down in the following ways: Some refused to voice their opinions and some distanced themselves socially and physically from those whom they perceived as better than themselves or those who showed no reciprocity in relationships.

Michelle Fine's (1992) research discussed silencing occurring in low-income public schools. Many teachers and administrators in Fine's research feared discussing issues relevant in the lives of the students and, as a result, silenced marginalized students and prevented them from connecting with school literacy. School for them became what Deborah Brandt (1990) has termed "the house of language-on-its-own." Fine's work uncovered and discussed a particular type of silencing—a hesitancy to name issues of concern. According to Fine, being able to name issues "involves those practices that facilitate critical conversation about social and economic arrangements, particularly about inequitable distributions of power and resources" (p. 120).

Silence, defined by Mary Belenky, Blythe Clinchy, Nancy Goldberger, and Jill Tarule (1986), represents "an extreme in denial of self and in dependence on external authority for direction" (p. 24). These authors state that silence reflects an absence of voice, and

> Although the silent women develop language, they do not cultivate their capacities for representational thought. They do not explore the power

that words have for either expressing or developing thought. Language is a tool for representing experience, and tools contribute to creative endeavors only when used. Language—even literacy—alone does not lead automatically to reflective, abstract thought (Scribner & Cole, 1981; Sigel & Cocking, 1977). In order for reflection to occur, the oral and written forms of language must pass back and forth between persons who both speak and listen or read and write—sharing, expanding, and reflecting on each other's experiences. Such interchanges lead to ways of knowing that enable individuals to enter into the social and intellectual life of their community. Without them, individuals remain isolated from others; and without tools for representing their experiences, people also remain isolated from the self. (pp. 25–26)

Many of the women I interviewed were silenced in this manner to a degree. However, their private journals and songs reveal an outpouring of emotion and an attempt to create self. But for most of the women, it is the interchange and reflection—and respect—that have been denied in literacy practices.

Brodkey's (1990) research revealed how middle-class discomfort with lower-class issues of daily life stopped the written communication attempts between human beings. In this work, Brodkey examined the correspondence of six middle-class teachers enrolled in a graduate course on teaching basic writing and six working-class women enrolled in an Adult Basic Education (ABE) class. She noted that the teachers found the letters stressful, and her examination revealed that the teachers "distanced and alienated" themselves from the ABE students "in their respective refusals to admit class concerns into the letters" (p. 294). I pondered this manuscript many times before and during my research, and I always wondered how the ABE students felt about writing and institutional literacy use when this distancing occurred. My own research participants, however, enlightened me. They told me how those of us who are educated, safely ensconced in middle- or upper-class worlds, shut out others. One white middle-class participant painfully admitted that she had distanced herself from others often based on class differences. She also admitted that she believed that her own background and ways of doing things were better. However, most of the women told me how they shut down and became silenced—after being shut out.

6

David Bleich (1988) noted the power of nonreciprocity while analyzing the research of Shirley Brice Heath and Amanda Branscombe. Heath and Branscombe (1985) urged high school research participants to write to Heath in addition to keeping field notes. When the participants were told that Heath, a well-educated and well-known ethnographer, would respond only to some participants, one young man demanded reciprocity. He asked Heath how she would feel if she wrote to someone who did not respond. He continued by asking Heath to "put [herself] in [their] shoes" (Heath & Branscombe, p. 24; as cited in Bleich, p. 320). Ellen Cushman (1996) also explored the importance of reciprocity in working with research participants; it creates respect and attempts to dispel any sense of being used by another person.

In Chapter 1, I discuss my own reflections about language, literacy, and arrogance. Chapter 2 briefly introduces the literacy ethnography that I conducted and the methodology involved. The recollections of the six women who participated in my research study focus primarily on reading, writing, and performance in the contexts of home, school, and church situated within and against regional and historical moments, for example, racial desegregation in the U.S. South and the Great Depression. Chapter 3 introduces the participants—Ella, Julia, Beverly, Sarah, Angel, and Edna—through their literacy history and recollections. Their experiences with shutdown in the areas of reading, writing, and performance continue to torment them and affect their participation in society, their choices in jobs, and their relationships with others. However, all of the women have resisted shutting down. In the last two stories, resisting shutdown as a consistent response to the arrogant perceptions of others emerges as a theme. In the concluding chapter, Chapter 4, I explore the desire by some persons to shut out others and the role of literacy in this exclusionary process. I also explore factors that seemed to help the women resist shutting down in terms of literacy use. The appendixes contain the interview questions I used in my qualitative research.

Arrogant perception seems to be the most powerful variable affecting shutting out, shutting down, and consequently, one's willingness to use language and literacy in U.S. culture. Shutting down, a response to being shut out, is often triggered by an interplay of arrogant perceptions based on many factors. Understanding our own arrogant perceptions is crucial to the reexamination of literacy, the institutions in which literacy is learned and used, and our often less-than-discerning interactions with others. Sacrificing these perceptions is what we must somehow do if those whom we teach are to grow.

The material aspects of our lives often are dictated by our perceptions of correctness: by our cars, clothes, and homes. In addition, our linguistic, cultural, and literacy capital is tied to our perceptions of correctness: in our manner of speaking, by the books we display and say we have read, and by our spelling proficiency, for example. Many people who come to believe that they are not correct will shut down. They will not dare reveal their literacy skills or linguistic repertoire in front of those whom they perceive as more correct. How many of our students shut down, choosing not to read and write in the presence of people they perceive as more correct or better educated? What role do teachers and those in positions of power—by virtue of complex and intersecting factors such as race, gender, and social class—play in causing others to shut down? Do those whom some perceive as correct, in fact, perceive themselves as more correct than others? If so, by what criteria do they judge themselves? What factors help people resist shutting down in the presence of those who may be perceived as correct? The literacy stories in this book begin to examine these questions, but they raise even more questions about literacy education in relation to powerful perceptions of correctness and arrogance.

CHAPTER 1

Language, Literacy, and Living: My Story

As a young girl growing up in rural North Carolina, I quickly realized that my mother spoke one language and my father spoke another. My mother came from a long line of well-educated people who read and quoted the great poets and the Bible. My father, on the other hand, came from poor, hard-working farmers and textile workers who frequently quoted the Bible and dutifully lived by their interpretations of it.

On weekends, my mother who was an English teacher, my father who was a farmer, and I would drive to nearby universities and see Shakespearean plays. On the way home in the car, I would chant, "Double, double, toil and trouble; Fire burn, and cauldron bubble," while my father and mother would discuss the themes and characters, and he would speak her language. On Sundays, we all went to the Methodist church my father attended as a child, a small church in the middle of rolling fields holding together the rural community of weather-worn farmers and textile workers. My parents' language changed subtly on Sundays, and they both spoke variations of southern regional dialect—especially in the afternoons when my father's brothers and sisters, who had not attended college, came to our house to visit my grandmother, who lived with us.

When I was older, I questioned my mother about this language shift and what I perceived as a dialectal hybridism. She answered that a truly educated person should be able to communicate with all people, that an education that does not allow one to speak humanely with a variety of people is not a complete education at all. She meant what she said, and she was respected in the rural community.

Reflecting on my personal experience with language, I realize that I always have been aware of its implications, its power, and its diversity. However, it was during my writing following the previously mentioned evening in Dr. Graves's class that a story from my childhood surfaced. I realized that it had shaped, powerfully yet subtly, my perceptions about social class, literacy, and my professional teaching decisions. That story became part of me the moment my father shared it with me.

Because my mother was not home from school when my school bus climbed the dirt road to our house, my father planned his farm work in order to meet me every day when I arrived home. One particular day, because of an incident at school, I dreaded seeing this compassionate man in overalls and straw hat waiting for me in the yard.

Earlier that day, after lunch, I had written a note to my best friend asking a question: "Do you hate B.B.? If yes, check the box."

Simply stated, B.B. was different. Older, taller, poorer—he had suddenly arrived from somewhere outside our safe, rural community. Sockless, he talked differently, and his clothes were dirty and torn. My friend, who obviously had listened to the morning devotional from *Guideposts*, marched promptly to my favorite teacher, Mrs. Mayo, and put the evidence of my sin on her desk. Mrs. Mayo read the note. Calmly, she told us to close our books, that she needed to tell us a story.

For a very long hour, she gently wove a fictional tale of hatred and arrogance, and love—a story that mirrored my insensitive letter and that convicted me of judging a person who appeared different. When the bell rang, Mrs. Mayo hugged me, and I fled. I held back the tears until I got off the bus. When I saw my father, he swooped me into his arms, and I knew that I was safe. But when I began to cry, he took my hand and suggested that we walk on the farm. I blurted out what I had done, and he listened. Like Mrs. Mayo, he did not chastise me. Finally, he sat on the steps and started recalling an event from his college days. As he talked, he looked over the fields, his eyes fixed on something that I could not see. I knew by heart, as we all did, the story of his attending college; it was a family legend. He was the only one in his family of 10 to attend college. As valedictorian of his high school class, he had been encouraged to further his education by my mother, who had been his high school English teacher. A resilient man, he farmed to work his way through college and, on the day he graduated, he asked my mother to marry him. They married, and I came along a few years later.

But on this day, he shared more than the legend; he shared his hurt. He had always loved literature, especially plays. On campus, he had seen a notice for play tryouts and worked up the courage to go, knowing he had never even been to a play.

"When I read the script," he told me, "they laughed. They laughed hard. They said that I was a country boy, and that, of course, I could not be in their play."

He took my hand then, and looked me in the eye as though I were an adult, and he told me never to make fun of a person's language or his or her poverty, for these things are part of the person. At that moment I understood my father's hurt but, I also learned that a country accent or dialect was dangerous. Speaking in this manner could shut out a person from certain institutions and groups of people. For years, I think that on many levels I resisted who I was and where I came from in spite of my father's advice. As I did with B.B., I shut others out of my life by distancing myself from them and their lives—their poverty and backgrounds—which, ironically, were probably not that different from my own. Later, I silenced discussion with which I might not have been comfortable in my classes. I learned to shed my southern accent and expressions on call. However, my father's story and my parents' strong insistence about not being arrogant resonated eventually, albeit painfully and slowly, and connected with my work in literacy and what has become my own heart-in-progress or personal growth.

When I graduated from college, I began my career as a vocational teacher and, immediately within the institutional hierarchy of the public school system, I received powerful messages from my colleagues that my students, who worked night shifts in textile mills, who bagged groceries, who washed dishes, were somehow not part of school life, as my colleagues perceived it. I visited the work sites and homes of my students and learned that most came from poor, working-class families. Many cared for parents plagued with serious health problems; many were minority students—and yet, they tried to stay in school and survive. However, it was this reality of daily survival that many of my middle-class colleagues did not want to recognize. Frankly, I found it hard to accept that some of my students slept in cars when their mothers were drunk or suddenly evicted, but I at least realized why they slept through 8 a.m. readings of *Julius Caesar*. These students lived a tragedy. Their life circumstances made some of my colleagues uncomfortable, and in early morning classes, my colleagues kept focused on reading and on studying the safe and distant tragedy that lived in texts, which could be opened and closed at will whether the students were asleep or not. I changed career paths out of frustration and maybe out of some deep desire to become more "correct." My students were marginalized, but as a vocational teacher, so was I.

No one has described more astutely the life of a vocational student than Rose (1990) in *Lives on the Boundary*. Rose had been tracked erroneously as a vocational student in high school but was lucky enough to be "redefined," as he puts it. Consequently, he has spent his life teaching and working with students "deemed slow or remedial or underprepared." In his book, he explores the defensive behavior and attitudes of many students tracked in schools: They take "on with a vengeance the identity implied in the vocational track" (p. 29). In fact, he suggests that many may "have to shut down" and "reject intellectual stimuli" because they believe the intellectual world is not available to them—or does not welcome them.

As I taught English and composition at the high school, community college, and university levels, I continued to note the social, material, and educational distance between many of my students, who were from low socioeconomic backgrounds or minority groups, and my colleagues. I also began to observe more keenly the power of language and the use of literacy in U.S. educational institutions to perpetuate distance by silencing or ignoring the communicative efforts of those who were trying to become educated according to cultural prescription. The irony struck me: Teachers and business leaders continued to declare that literacy acquisition—being able to read and write—was necessary for social and financial mobility. Yet I frequently observed literacy teachers using their literacy and oral communication skills to shut out the very persons who could have benefited most from these teachers' willingness to connect with them through literacy and discourse. Unfortunately, those whom I have observed shutting out others either were completely unaware of the implications of the interaction or were so arrogant or fearful that they felt compelled by virtue of race, position, education, or class to shut out others.

In a discussion of arrogant perception, Lugones (1987) suggests that we may be trained to be arrogant perceivers of those with whom we do not wish to identify, and that we may be the objects of this perception across lines of racial, gender, and cultural boundaries. In the subsequent chapters, the women I interviewed talk about this learned arrogance, and they show us how they relate it to literacy and language in the important "shaping" institutions of home, church, and school. Some of the women tell us how they have dealt with arrogance.

I wonder how many readers, momentarily, made note that I had been a vocational teacher, an admission that may have made some readers uncomfortable regarding my credibility as an English teacher. And if those readers were totally honest, I am sure that some of them were distanced at that moment of transaction with my words, words that simply represented a segment of my life. If anyone was distanced momentarily, what stereotypical perceptions created the distance? What feelings and beliefs colored those perceptions? Was it a perception of arrogance based on deeply ingrained beliefs about education, intellect, or class?

The words of Kurt Spellmeyer (1993) validated the story told to me by my father:

> to silence any person, to prohibit his speech or discredit his manner of speaking, is therefore to silence much more than the person, not only everyone from whom the speaker learned his words, but also everything these words have made real" (p. 269).

In my father's story, I heard what his words had "made real" on several levels. I heard the story of a powerful language experience and the impact of this experience on him. His recollection also illuminated my own understanding of my family, my identity in relation to them, and the place where I lived in relation to a larger world.

Many people do not recover from experiences like the one my father recounted. As Rose (1990) stated, they may not be lucky enough to be "redefined." They go on with life, but many begin to believe that they are inferior or unworthy somehow, because they have been judged by others—before connecting with others. The judgmental voices of others become part of their memories and influence dreams and choices. They have been shut off from reading, writing, and performing in various contexts often because those in power sent signals that they themselves were superior and that their worlds were off limits. All too often appropriate books, correct writing, and proper speech signal an appropriate background, one perceived to be better and reflecting higher standards. Those not possessing this background can respond in a variety of ways. The stories you will read suggest that not everyone can procure this background readily or easily, and that not everyone wishes to. We also see that acquiring this background can sever a person from his or her family and values, which are often quite valuable.

Moments of retreating into silence or realizing that one has been shut out are rarely forgotten. I believe that at the moment that distance or silence is established between people, it is internalized, becoming part of one's identity and shaping one's attitudes about oneself, about those assumed to be superior, and about the institution in which the encounter occurred. Shutdown in relation to literacy affects one's perception of the value of literacy and the communicative acts of reading, writing, speaking, and listening in one's life. The stories in this book raise questions about arrogant perceptions and show the subtle ways we use literacy to perpetuate distance and resist human connection.

CHAPTER 2

Conducting a Literacy Ethnography: Hearing How People Feel

Rethinking Literacy Research

During the last several decades, literacy research has gone beyond traditional boundaries, and researchers now are exploring new models of literacy that address aspects of culture and power inherent in literacy practices in various cultural and situational contexts. The work of Mina Shaughnessy, Shirley Brice Heath, Denny Taylor, and Mike Rose, for example, drew attention to the socio-ideological nature of institutional and community discourses. They alerted us that many persons traveling from everyday life to institutional school life could not shed easily or quickly their lives and their language for on-the-spot command performances under the direction of some English teachers who may have been "elitist without apology," according to Spellmeyer (1996). In fact, in order to be accepted in various institutions, one had to learn the language and literacy background demanded, or one would be shut out. Assimilation is not always so tidy, however.

Current research is focusing on reexamining literacy within the culture and on understanding the power of rapidly changing literacy within and across contexts and time periods. However, more innovative research is needed that simply asks people about the intersection of their language and their use of literacy: how their language and literacy experiences have been nurtured or discredited and how they have chosen to respond, as a result. Many literacy specialists advocate allowing research participants to speak (LeCompte, 1993; Moss, 1994; Street, 1993), and some researchers are beginning to ask the opinions of

> those who are the object of much discussion and debate—members of nonmainstream communities where literacy practices may or most likely may not match literacy practices in mainstream academic communities. These are the voices that have been missing from so much of the previous research on literacy. (Moss, 1994, p. 2)

It is fledgling research that attempts to dislodge power and bias and not give way to "a type of free touching of the power-less by the power-full" (Royster, 1996, p. 32). When I heard the participants in my study explain their feelings about reading, writing, and speaking in the contexts of home, school, and church, I began to sense and understand the far-reaching implications of being the objects of arrogant perception across time and place. I also began to understand the implications of being an arrogant perceiver of others. Arrogance creates an invisible barrier affecting one's freedom to use literacy in its most basic forms; it is a force field preventing people from reading, writing, and speaking. Arrogant perceptions are insidious, sneaking into even the most well-intended and open interchanges. During my final meetings with some of the women, they made it clear that although they had participated in the research and reviewed the transcripts, I was the author, one they perceived as more correct with words than themselves and one who still had ultimate power. Even though I had allowed the women to speak, it was my voice that was going to be heard.

By listening to the women talk and transcribing their recollections, I realized that literacy stories often triggered other memories, perhaps not seemingly related to literacy. However, it was this powerful interconnectedness of literacy to the details of existence and survival that struck me. In Ella's story, for example, she felt compelled to describe the foods she ate while growing up. She was well aware that these foods marked her status as "country" and southern. As she talked, I realized that this everyday vocabulary of life is part of us, and for many people, it does not match the vocabulary of the world of Sally, Dick, and Jane, literacy figures that Ella recalled from her school experience. I saw that each of the women was quite capable of seeing literacy's impact in her life, although most admitted that they had never been made aware of it before. Perhaps it is those of us who lay claim to teaching it—Royster's "power-full"—who do not grasp its far-reaching and subtle effects. Perhaps we do not understand the vocabulary lists of real lives; perhaps some of these lists are not correct in our minds because of our backgrounds.

It is after this research and years of teaching that I am beginning to grasp the power of "being correct." When Sarah recalled the humiliation of misspelling words publicly in "demeaning" spelling bees and receiving red-inked papers fraught with errors, she revealed that she never applied for jobs requiring writing because her imperfections might be revealed. Another woman, Beverly, who had been a teacher, realized in painful self-exploration during the study that she had been taught to "perceive arrogantly." She was aware of the dissonance in her stated religious beliefs and her sometimes arrogant feelings about others, and she saw the line of questioning as an opportunity to grow. After much discussion and exploration, we attributed the dissonance to an attitude of arrogance learned within her wealthy and well-educated family of origin, her private school, and her husband's profession. She admitted painfully that she often had perceived her own background as one reflecting higher standards when meeting people whose way of doing things, dress and possessions, and manner of speech differed from her own. Interestingly, she confessed that she had never been a good reader—a fast reader—at school and, knowing that she could never reveal this difficulty to her peers, she avoided situations in which she would be found out—by other well-educated persons of her own social class. When her friends suggested forming book groups, she made excuses for not joining them rather than reveal a perceived inadequacy.

Much research has explored causes for reading and writing failure and causes for illiteracy. A host of fragmented variables from one's background continues to emerge, including income level, parental educational levels, and race and ethnicity. Recently, the variables' intersecting nature has been explored (Hourigan, 1994; Lubeck, 1988; Rockhill, 1993; Snow, Barnes, Chandler, Goodman, & Hemphill, 1991). This direction is positive, for unfortunately the variables have emerged frequently to paint portraits of at-risk people, people who perhaps, in the words of the participant just mentioned, have backgrounds that are different from those of many mainstream U.S. citizens. Regardless of the direction of research, however, I think we have overlooked what I believe to be the root of the problem. Lugones (1987) stated, "To the extent that we learn to perceive others arrogantly or come to see them only as products of arrogant perception and continue to perceive them that way, we fail to identify with them—fail to love them" (p. 4). Our own arrogant perceptions of others are based on the variables we continue to examine and ponder; we fail, however, to examine and ponder the power of our own perceptions to affect the lives of others in relation to literacy use.

Spellmeyer (1996) stated that English teachers must "become ethnographers of *experience*," ethnographers who are not just "armchair readers of the 'social text,' but scholar/teachers who find out how people actually *feel*" (p. 911). As I began my participatory ethnographic research with the best intentions, I set out to do just that. However, I quickly learned that this posture is still somewhat presumptuous. Finding out how others feel does us no good if we are not willing as "scholar/teachers" to examine how we feel about those who may be the objects of our own arrogant perceptions.

Conducting the Interviews

Working from a critical analytical framework, I wrote a series of intensive life-history interview questions (Belenky et al., 1986) that focused on literacy- and language-related experiences in home, school, and church. Before beginning the research, I answered my own questions. Then with the approval of pastors of two racially and socioeconomically diverse churches, I issued invitations for participation in my research at church meetings. I made it clear that I wanted the participants' help in getting my Ph.D. and that participating would be time consuming.

I asked for no preliminary survey information; I wanted to impose neither categorical labels nor language, which might influence the participants in their interview responses. I did not want any preliminary variables, such as age, income level, or marital status, influencing my interactions with them or my analysis of their literacy stories. I knew that if I prompted them with survey questions and boxes to check that I would be creating a barrier using literacy. Forms would reveal personal information—race, educational level, and income—which to many persons, when evaluated by others in power, would permanently label them. Therefore, I decided to begin with conversation, which would become the text from which we would work.

Six women, three African American and three white, ranging in age from 40 years to 70 years, participated in the study. At the time of the study, one woman was widowed, two were married, and three were divorced. All participants were mothers, and three were grandmothers. All had been born and reared in the southern United States except one participant who grew up in a northeastern city. All the women had moved from their place of birth to the cosmopolitan area in which they were residing at the time of the study. All were high school graduates. One was a college graduate, and three participants had taken some college level courses. Although all the women in the study had been employed previously, only two were employed at the time of the study.

Initially, I met with each volunteer at her home or mine to discuss the project. This meeting was not rushed and was necessary to establish rapport, sincerity, and trust. I moved slowly, spending a great deal of time over coffee just talking about church, children, and pets. Eventually, I explained and read aloud the consent form, and I worked with each woman to select a pseudonym and explained why a pseudonym was necessary. Most of the women who volunteered had little knowledge of academic research; they did not know its vocabulary, so I explained carefully the purposes of the interviews and my obligation to respect their privacy.

Then I showed them the series of questions that they would be asked, and I explained that I would tape-record their responses and our dialogue. We spent a lot of time practicing tape recording, just getting comfortable hearing our voices. Ella was so frightened at revealing her southern accent that she refused to be taped until the second interview. When I explained to Ella that I would like to tape record our interviews, she laughed nervously and said that her accent was "southern, southern, southern, southern!" She added, "I'm probably more self-conscious about my grammar than my accent." So I wrote by hand her responses to the first interview. After the first interview, she became more comfortable and soon agreed to be tape recorded.

I explained to all the participants that I would return the transcripts to them prior to each meeting for their review. After the initial interview, each subsequent interview was preceded by a discussion of the transcript of the previous session. However, Ella returned her first transcriptions with no written markings. Instead, she had *silently* marked passages with sticky notes. When I asked her what these notes meant—if she wanted me to delete the passages—she looked at me, laughed, and stated emphatically that these passages revealed too much of her dialect and that I was simply to fix the grammar. I agreed to do so without eliminating colloquialisms. She wanted to keep her transcripts as records of family history and to be proud of them; she wanted typed records to be correct. With the exception of Ella's first interview, I transcribed all the interviews verbatim using a transcribing machine.

Many of the women were surprised at their role in the review process, and this aspect of involvement seemed to prove to them that I valued their input and their right to rethink, clarify, and delete their thoughts as they appeared on paper. Brian Street (1993) argued for ethnographic research in the area of literacy that allows researchers to encourage the active participation of those who use literacy in their daily lives. He believed that researchers should not remain trapped by methodologies that assume "supposedly passive recipients" of literacy skills. I also shared that I had answered all the questions myself and, although I had to be careful about not monopolizing conversation, the women seemed pleased that I had been willing to do what I was asking them to do. The conversational aspect of the "nonscheduled" interviews (Denzin, 1978) at first disturbed two white, middle-class participants who seemed to want me to control and direct their responses; they wanted me to be sure we followed the questions as I had typed them. The same interview questions were asked of all participants; however, they were not necessarily asked in the same order. The women's responses did not lend themselves always to a neat question-answer scenario, and I frequently jumped from one set of questions to another, although I made sure that all questions were addressed eventually. These same two participants, in particular, seemed to think that there were correct responses to some of the questions but, as their own self-analyses reflected, they seemed pleased that they eventually overcame this fear about having to respond *correctly* and *in order*. The women, I think, enjoyed having their thoughts valued, and they enjoyed being invited to discuss literacy practices in relation to their lives, the complexities of which are not often addressed in literacy research.

During a period of 6 months, I met with each woman at least 6 times for 2-hour sessions; some sessions were longer. Between appointments, I frequently visited their homes and dropped off transcripts, and we often talked by phone. They frequently initiated calls to me to recount other stories they had remembered since our last meeting or to share and discuss a literacy encounter experienced recently. During the research period, I saw these women in various community settings, and although I did not use participant-observation as part of my methodology, I mentioned in their stories any literacy-related observations that both the participants and I felt might be helpful or appropriate.

Respectively, each set of questions focused on the following: past and present life circumstances; reading, writing, and performance at home; reading, writing, and performance at school; reading, writing, and performance at church; and discussion of the participant's feelings about the research process. Additional conversations and interviews focused on my specific concerns or those of the participants and their reactions to the transcripts. Although the questions were categorized according to cultural context, the transcribed responses revealed what Brandt (1995) described as "interpenetration and overlapping of influences as people criss-cross among various literacy-based institutions in the course of their normal lives" (p. 666). Although the interview transcriptions make up the bulk of the data, my field notes, the participants' audiotaped reactions to transcripts, and my analyses also serve to triangulate the data. Some participants readily shared favorite books, treasured essays, and photos. These artifacts are referenced in the stories; however, I chose not to copy and include any of these artifacts to protect the identity of the participants.

As the participants and I got better acquainted through the interviews, I helped participants with letters, résumés, and family history writing. I was quite conscious of being honest about my graduate work and about reciprocating appropriately. All participants received copies of their transcripts, and several told me that they were honored to be participants. Two women told me that they wanted me to

21

"make it" and that they were glad to help. In the early stages of the research, several stated that they were afraid their lives were not interesting enough for the study or they had no idea that anything in their life experience could be helpful or worthy of notice. But through our dialogues, they seemed to become more assured that their experiences had value. Eventually, all the women stated that participating was a way to give something to the world and to the future.

Analyzing the Process

In my preliminary discussions with the women who came forward to participate, I believe that I connected with them because of my own varied background—my rural past and my travels. With each woman, I shared a common religious faith. We always sat on the floor or around kitchen tables in their homes or mine. Edna stated that she felt that I had "a way of questioning people and without realizing it, *they* divulged truths in some things that they haven't divulged to their closest friends." She prefaced the statement as a compliment, but it made me wonder; her pronoun lapse from *I* to *they* was the first such lapse in approximately 70 pages of transcriptions, suggesting to me that she was not completely comfortable with her admissions to me. Did my role as a researcher, a Ph.D. candidate, create a barrier that could not be removed?

They all revealed a great deal of personal information, which at times distanced me—"the mother, the military wife, and the Christian"—words from my own interview transcript that defined me. Sometimes I did not understand a participant's story or episode; sometimes I disagreed with or disapproved of a participant's behavior. At these moments, I had to continue interviewing, to continue being the objective and professional researcher, and to continue probing. But when I got home, I reviewed my own transcripts and examined who might be resisting identification—or in Lugones's words, failing to love. I then transcribed the interview tapes and noted any troubling dialogue. I had to examine how I felt before trying to understand or attempting to analyze how the participants felt. Because of my own background, was I arrogantly perceiving another person? I chose to acknowledge my own limitations as one whose "own experience and personal history, including [my]…cultural, social, and familial frame of reference, may shape how [I listen] and what [I hear]" (Taylor, Gilligan, & Sullivan, 1995, p.14). Acknowledging these limitations was neither pleasant nor easy.

I confronted my instinct to shut out by distancing or disapproving of another person by noting it following the interview, reflecting on the matter, and discussing it with the participant in question at the next interview session. I also resisted an instinct to shut down and not name the issue, because ignoring an issue by retreating into silence would have been more comfortable, more safe. Instead I explained my reaction (confusion, surprise, and judgment)[1] to certain passages, and why I thought that I had the reaction. I talked about the factors in my own background that could have caused it. When I invited response, the resulting self-analysis and discussion seemed to assure some participants of my authenticity. However, the same two women who wanted to give me "correct" answers also wanted an objective researcher to direct the study's agenda. By admitting my own perceptions, I was coming across as less than perfect and was not living up to their perceptions of a Ph.D. candidate who should know the answers. Initially, these women readily deferred to my educational advantage and were not comfortable when I tried to juggle power and initiate uncomfortable dialogue.

For example, Beverly and I discussed an example of arrogant perception from a Christian frame of reference, which I had chosen as a common context to examine a portion of her transcript. When I told her that I planned to reveal in the dissertation my reaction to the scenario based on my religious beliefs, she expressed concern for me. She said I should be more professional and objective and not mention that we had discussed the scenario from a common, religious, vantage point. She feared my "naming" my religious beliefs to an academic audience might jeopardize my degree. However, I argued that finding a connecting factor from which to name the issue under consideration seemed to be the key to initiating and sustaining the dialogue. As Margaret LeCompte and Judith Preissle (1993) state, "subjective reactions and responses are often sources for methodological decisions" (p. 92–93). I was cautious about not using confrontational or morally chastising tactics. Instead I would find a common and appropriate frame of reference through which to initiate exploration and discussion. But when I chose to de-elevate myself, I obviously up-

23

set the assumed hierarchal structure of a researcher-participant relationship and middle-class educational expectations.

During the final interviews, I asked the women to evaluate my analyses and to describe the research process as they had experienced it. I showed Sarah some visual displays of the data: a cognitive map highlighting her literacy experiences within the contexts of home, school, and church; and a causal display focusing on her experiences with shutdown, the factors that had contributed to them, and her responses to them in relation to literacy and language. Sarah liked these pictures, and she uncharacteristically asked for a pencil to draw and make notes on them. She commented as she worked that it was easier to argue with me using pictures; she added that marking my written analyses was difficult because she knew that as an English teacher I was an authority with words. Although her words had contributed to the text of my work, I was still the "power-full." Beverly made a similar comment, noting that I was the expert in grammar.

Julia and Sarah are savvy; both chided me good-naturedly about my Ph.D. But both knew and showed me that while I am struggling to write and voice opinions—their opinions and mine—they are still silenced somewhat because I am the writer, the one who is an expert on grammar. My education is still a ticket to power, which comes with a robe of arrogance, if I choose to don it.

I hope that some of the women in this study found that the research process and transcription review can lead to "connection over separation, understanding and acceptance over assessment, and collaboration over debate" (Belenky et al., 1986, p. 229). I still keep in touch with them, and they continue to teach me about language, literacy, arrogance, and power. I greatly respect each woman's courage, honesty, and willingness to grow.

CHAPTER 3

Language, Literacy, and Living: The Women's Recollections

The literacy stories recounted in this chapter are the stories of Ella, Julia, Beverly, Sarah, Angel, and Edna. As you read these accounts, you will feel connected to some of the women and distanced from others—but safely distanced because I have introduced you to them in the safe world of text. I believe these stories can teach us if we allow ourselves to examine how we perceive others and if we listen to how the women feel about literacy, background, and power in U.S. culture. I believe we must hear the vocabulary of their worlds and train ourselves to note the moments when literacy is integral to their daily existence and struggles. Some details from their lives may not seem to have any bearing on literacy practices, but I believe these details will affect you as readers in shaping a perception of these women—a practice of which you may not be aware and one in which you may engage when listening to your students read or reading their journals.

Some of the women will recount moments of feeling shut out, and they will describe the act of shutting down. Others will recount moments of feeling that they were objects of arrogant perception. Some of the women will resist these moments and continue on, much like my father. They will continue to read, write, and voice their opinions. But a shadow of arrogance will prevail over certain institutions and the people in them who are in charge of appropriate literacy and correct language usage—a powerful shadow casting itself across time and space.

The extensive transcripts from which the stories were derived were overwhelming and unwieldy. Thus, as a framework, I have chosen to recount highlights of each participant's literacy history. Details about each participant's life have been modified to protect their anonymity, and each woman is introduced by a pseudonym. The literacy vignettes incorporate some of the participants' past and present life circumstances, self-description, and recollections of literacy- and language-related experiences at home, church, and school. Sometimes I "comment, reflect, and analyze," in the words of Mike Rose (1990, p. xxi), for I, too, don't "know how else to get it right." Italicized words in quoted material reflect the speaker's emphasis of these words during our interviews. Moments of literacy shutdown and success are interwoven into the narratives.

I have chosen not to group the participants by race, age, or any assumed social class level; I believe it is wiser to meet them introduced randomly as we chance upon each other in life. I prefer not to use the term "case-by-case analysis" because of a lesson I learned during the research from Julia, who I believe will teach all of us in positions of power—"bigwigs and Ph.D.s" who might have noble intentions, but perhaps arrogant perceptions—quite a bit about "cases."

As the stories have unfolded during my writing and analysis, I have found that their juxtaposition has led me to attempt to introduce them "safely" to one another. For example, after introducing Ella, I may mention her in someone else's story, contrasting or comparing an experience. Therefore, I recommend reading the stories in the order presented. The first two stories of Ella and Julia reveal similar life circumstances. Both women perceive themselves to be shut out from certain worlds because of racial and socioeconomic oppression, and both are hesitant to reveal their language usage and literacy skills in front of educated or correct people. Both women are fighters, however, and both have had moments when they have had to resist being shut out. The next two stories of Beverly and Sarah focus on the literacy experiences of middle-class women who were raised in affluent circumstances. These women have often shut down for fear of being perceived by those in their own social class as less than perfect, less than correct. Trained to *perform properly*, they have often feared not living up to the expectations demanded by those of their social class status. The last two women introduced, Angel and Edna, have consistently refused to shut down—even when feeling shut out. Both were raised by single mothers and came from poor backgrounds. Both of these women have used literacy—reading and writing—to improve their life circumstances, and both seem to have acquired quite early in life Dahl and Freppon's (1995) "disposition for learning." They believe they have a right to use literacy, to ask questions, and to speak; learning for them is not a passive school-related activity.

Admittedly, if I had arranged these stories in another order, I may have seen other patterns. In future research I would like to continue collecting stories from men and women who struggle with English as a second language. In our English classes, we rarely have this kind of opportunity, for we are too busy assessing and grading literacy performance in an institution that some of these women believe is quite detached from real life.

Ella's Story

Ella, a 40-year-old African American, was born in a small southern rural community where she and her family worked in fields of cotton and beans. Her father was a carpenter when the weather permitted, but both parents plowed behind mules, and the children followed behind and hoed. "When we were little," she stated, "we weren't really poor. We had food, clothes. Mama made sure that we had clothes and shoes. We always managed. We were not *poor-poor-poor* because Mama made sure that our hair was washed, our clothes pressed clean. *Love went into that.* We ate red beans, black-eyed peas, fried okra, and sweet potatoes. We didn't really want for anything. And yet there were times when my parents didn't have any money, like Christmas, but when Christmas came, we still had something. But I always had this butterfly in the pit of my stomach, because I thought we wouldn't get anything for Christmas."

Raised in a Christian home, Ella states that Christianity is her "character"; it is instilled in her. Her father had a fifth-grade education; her mother, a sixth-grade education. Ella, however, graduated from high school and attended a racially desegregated school for the first time in high school. Although proud of some aspects of her rural heritage, Ella disliked field life, and hated what she termed "the darkness of the South."

"The darkness of the South," explained Ella, came from an incredibly strong sense of place and time, and was influenced by "the talk, the talk of parents putting fear in me." Ella described this darkness: "I was scared at night, for the coons would come out to eat the chickens. The dogs would be carrying on, hollering, and bucking. I was afraid of the South. Lynchings. A black man stepped out of place one time. A 15-year-old boy. He had stopped on the road to pick up a girl's book that she had dropped. But she went home and told her parents. They came and had him castrated in his front yard. Thought he was making a pass at her. Now I didn't *see* any of this. But the *talk*. The *talk* of parents put fear in me."

After she graduated from high school, Ella married, got pregnant, and left her home. However, she found her accent to be an obstacle to friendships and acceptance. She eventually moved again to the cosmopolitan southern city where she now resides. She stated that not furthering her education is a regret, but when younger, she did not believe that she had the ability to go on to school. She recalled that her third-grade teacher and family said, "That Ella is going to be somebody. When I didn't go to college, I let them down. I believed I wasn't college material." When she and her husband divorced, she did not believe that she could be on her own with her children, but she told me, "God gave me wisdom and showed me how to save money." Having put one child through college, Ella is proud of her independence.

The tom-boy child who was always smiling and playing and singing is now a woman who is outspoken in some ways but silenced in other ways. She is highly sensitive to unkindness and harshness. Overcoming health problems and rearing her children alone have been major challenges, and her sensitivity to her accent has increased during this time of change in her life. She refused to be audiotaped during the first interview because she was so uncomfortable about her accent and grammar. She even asked me if her accent was the "*real*" reason that I wanted to interview her. In retrospect, I wonder if I was actually drawn to her in some ways because of it.

When Ella was growing up in the South, her accent was not a problem at home with her family. She perceived her community, her church, and her school, until high school, as "family." Everybody "talked the same way," and "everybody fit in." Her accent bothered her, however, when she "ventured into a *big city*," and people commented, "Where are you from? You have a *southern* accent!" Even when she attended school with white children in the South, her accent was not a problem. It became a problem in a cosmopolitan area, where language usage is judged more along class lines than racial lines.

She stated her belief that in order to survive, African Americans and whites from the South "somehow learn to talk properly" when they come to a city, and then they "put *you* down." One friend, originally from a northern city, made her terribly "uncomfortable." During conversations, her friend would "mark" Ella's words—in mid-sentence. Then her friend's children would laugh at the verbal exchange. Ella stated that this friend spoke in a "very distinguished manner." The relationship deteriorated, however, for after these exchanges, the friend would drop by only when "she was down and out." Language arrogance, relating to composite regional, educational, and class perceptions created a gulf, and soon Ella disassociated or distanced herself from this woman. The woman failed to respect Ella's feelings and condoned the laughter of her children; she gave no kindness, and she, in turn, received none. Ella's child also corrects her speech and says that she speaks in a "country" manner. This child told Ella, "You people from the country just don't pronounce your words right. So I'm glad I'm not from there because I don't want to speak like that." This child is being educated in the city but has heard Ella's stories of growing up in the country.

Generally, Ella's parents did not read, but she read her school books to them—her mother exhibiting more patience in listening than her father. Her mother, however, read the Bible, "which was a must." The Bible and school books were the only printed materials in the house. Ella and her brothers and sisters played school and church on the front porch of their house. Her brothers always assumed the role of preacher; Ella and her sisters became teachers who "would have the others read." Ella remembered a sibling squirming with an easy verse in church and not being able to pronounce the word *faithfulness*. Ella vividly recalled her mother's embarrassment when her mother realized in a public setting that her child could not read well.

Ella's current home has lovely bookcases filled with encyclopedias, books, and magazines. She recalled reading aloud to her own children, who would snuggle in bed with her. They had a favorite story about a frisky animal, and she stated, "They could tell you this story inside out." She read it over and over until it was "coming out their ears." Ella likes to read her Bible at home now, but she confided that she had always been embarrassed reading out loud in front of strangers.

Our discussion of writing prompted Ella to leave the room momentarily to secure a box of papers from which she pulled an essay written by her daughter when she was in high school. This piece of writing is treasured by Ella, for it proves to her that some of her values have been transmitted to her daughter. In the essay her daughter gives her mother credit for instilling in her a belief in herself, a belief that she must not depend on anything or anyone other than herself in life—not males, not welfare, not luck. Her daughter describes herself as a "black American and a female," a combination of traits, she states, which will not keep her from succeeding—regardless of stereotypical perceptions. Ella and her daughter are highly aware of the "triple jeopardy" situations (class, racial, and gender oppression) in which African American women frequently find themselves, as discussed by Marsha Houston Stanback (1988). Ella stated succinctly that the essay focused on being a "black American and also a female—*that puts her in the lowest category of society—whom they refer to as minorities.*" Ella's perceptions of these traits, in addition to perceiving herself as country and southern, often make her believe that she is shut out, distanced from others who are better educated in society. Her daughter, Ella shared, was told by high school teachers and counselors that she was not "college material." However, Ella's daughter refused to shut down and, in essence, be shut out from the world of higher education. Ella believes it was the essay, lovingly taken from a box and shared with me, which won her daughter college acceptance, a degree, and a career.

The essay is a confirmation to Ella that her values have been passed on. Ella and I both cried when we read it. She said, "I know from reading it again that she's going to make it." The interrelationship between the act of speaking, listening, writing, and reading is salient in this recollection. This literacy artifact has meaning far beyond its original purpose, and it lives across time in the life and pride of this family. Ella's third-grade teacher, whom she adored, made her internalize these words: *Be proud of who you are. Be proud of what you are. Be proud of what you stand for.* These oral lessons eventually wove their way into the essay produced by Ella's daughter and helped keep both Ella and her daughter from shutting down when people in power attempted to shut them out. Ella keeps a journal for herself, and she said, "I would *someday* like to pass it on to my daughter, *just to let my daughter know my thoughts and know me.*" Words taking a permanent form have the power, in Ella's mind, to define her or perhaps, as Mike Rose suggested, to redefine her.

Ella writes letters to friends and family members. She also frequently uses letter writing to express her opinions to school and government officials; however, she noted that she writes these business letters "with friends." At this point in our discussion, she expressed distance from me when she stated, "I don't write like you." She explained, "Your writing is very professional, and my writing is scribble, scrabble on a piece of paper."

"Ella, why do you think your writing is scribble, scrabble?" I asked.

She said that her handwriting was "*terrible*," and she compared it to mine and her sister's. She added that she spells better now than she used to because she has "a little electronic thing that will spell words" for her. She explained her writing process: "I used to stop, run get a dictionary, and then my thoughts—I would lose my thoughts!"

"How would you feel if I saw some of your writing and you had misspelled a word?" I continued.

She quickly stated, "If a friend saw it, somebody who was *used* to me, I wouldn't feel bad. If a friend saw it, I wouldn't take it to heart. But if *you* saw it, I would really feel terrible because you're *correct*, and I wouldn't want you to know that I didn't know how to spell that word."

When she said this, it took me a moment to focus, to keep the dialogue moving. I was overcome with sadness. Ella kept her eyes focused on me. Finally I said, "You gotta be honest. Is it my education?"

Ella said, "Probably so. I'm very skeptical about people who are well educated, who are better educated than I am. It makes me sad—because it just shows you're—*southern. It just shows who you are and where you come from. I think it's being—southern. Southern is always a put-down.*"

Ella is a religious woman; she knows Bible stories, quotes scriptures, and she uses them to explain everyday situations. Indeed, it seems that, as she stated, Christianity is instilled in her, part of her character. "When I was growing up," she said, "I heard things that white people did to black people, and those things made me angry and bitter towards white people. As I got older, I kept saying why do white people think they are superior to us? God made us all. We're human beings; we're all people. I focus on Jesus, and even as a teenager, I kept focused on who I was." This focus that she is loved and valued by Jesus helps keep her going, helps her refute, at least verbally, an arrogance by white people that she knows in her heart is wrong.

Growing up, she attended a country church. Her family frequently walked many miles to the services, sometimes catching a ride with a neighbor. When they entered the church, everyone knew one another: deacons, shouting sisters, the choir members, and the preacher. The preaching was powerful. Ella recalled one preacher who made quite an impression on her: His sermons made her "hair stand up." Hearing him talk about the Book of Revelation, she was so scared that she "scooted down in the seat." She noted that even though he had a "sweet voice" at times, he scared her even when he wasn't discussing the Book of Revelation. So powerful was this man's storytelling ability and communicative skill that she noted, "His sermons always stood in my mind. If I didn't live right, I would not enter the Kingdom."

Ella remembered no significant writing done at church, but she did read verses in Sunday school. She recalled a small Testament that she kept hidden in her pocketbook. The little book was a treasure, something she hid because, she explained, there were so many children in her family that she was afraid one of her brothers or sisters would take it. However, rather than reading, it is performance that Ella recalled so fondly. The church was what Mary Louis Pratt (1991) referred to as a "safe house." Everyone talked the same in this place; the vocabulary revealed experiences shared and understood from historical, economic, and social perspectives. An older lady in the church encouraged "*all the children*" to sing in the choir, and Ella, who has a beautiful voice, did sing. No one was shut out. At first "shy and bashful," she attended choir practice and eventually led songs. She also loved "doing speeches" and recalled the third chapter of Ecclesiastes and recited part of it during our interview. Everyone had a part in all programs and plays at church, for it was a "family thing." At church, unlike at school, she could be herself; if someone missed a line in a church play, the director just "whispered it to you."

School was different. Ella recalled in the fourth grade a woman coming to her school and telling the children to memorize John 3:16. Obviously, each child later had to compete and recite it in front of the woman in order to win a Bible, which was the prize. Ella stated emphatically that she wanted that Bible and that she learned the verse; however, she did not get it—*"because there was someone else better than me!"* Competition, in terms of being better than someone else, was an integral part of school life.

Church is still a central part of Ella's life. She now attends a large urban church where she is, in some ways, an "outsider" because she was not born in the area. When she stops in during the week, she is "stopped by secretaries at the door." Preaching and sharing testimonials dominate the service. She participates in small groups and Bible studies in which she feels comfortable, groups that she likened to "families." She teaches Sunday school for children, but she does not feel called to sing in the choir at this new church: Its choir loft is quite high and imposing.

Ella demonstrated that she was highly aware of what people say about her accent; each comment seemed permanently etched in her mind. Her ex-husband, who did not grow up in the country, and her sister have chided her, stating, "Ella's still dragging because she still has it." She added that when she is in church and speaking, if she perceives that anyone is laughing or smirking, that she will "just stop and sit down." She believes that people don't tune in to her and don't listen to her opinion because of how they perceive her accent. She therefore hates participating in some groups because her "voice is not being heard." She describes many members of her current church as people who "have degrees, have titles, or have something"; they are "in charge" and have been for many years. Upon reflecting, she stated that she is "probably more self-conscious about [her] grammar than [her] accent." Her perception of her accent and grammar and its probable reception by people who speak "properly" carries over into her comfort with writing, reading, and public performance. Her current church is not quite a safe house, according to Pratt's definition; its African American congregation is economically and educationally diverse. These factors can create distance; those educated speak properly, and they rise to positions of power. They dictate the use of written materials.

Ella described the two schools she attended in the 1950s and 1960s: her segregated elementary school and her desegregated high school. She did not begin attending the "little country school" until she was seven because her mother could not find her birth certificate—a document dictating her right to begin school. The elementary school had sliding doors that separated the grades, an outhouse, and outdoor water. Lunch was cooked in a little room, and at mealtime boys carried trays to the classrooms where the children ate. Adjacent to Ella's school was a "big, beautiful white school."

In describing her first experiences with school reading, Ella commented, "We used the books when the white kids were through with them." She noted laughingly that having used books did not make her feel bad *because they were books, and I enjoyed books! Books are books!*" And then she recalled, "The books weren't really raggedy, and I couldn't understand why we were given those books. They were a little ragged, a little torn, but you know, you know, Daphne, how white people are: If the books start to look ragged or a little torn, *they've* got to get rid of them. *We* kept them until they fell apart and until we couldn't use them anymore." Ella commented on this phenomenon of conspicuous consumption now affecting many people in their continual quest to have "better-than-you things."

Ella basically learned to read on her own; she never learned to "take a word and break it into syllables"—syllabication skills being some of the "basics" she missed. Of her early reading in school, she instantly recalled: *Run Sally Run Down Down Down Up Up Up Sally I And Me. Simple words."* Reading got harder for Ella in the third grade, and "following along when [the children] read aloud seemed to help." Her parents didn't help her with homework, for "they didn't know—like parents now—to help with homework. And at the end of their physically exhausting days, they slept." However, her third-grade teacher, a quiet, demanding woman who talked softly, did help her after school. Ella "trusted" this woman and felt her "warmth." Ella said that, in her own mind, when she read, she "dragged." She would stop and try "to break the word up," but ultimately she "just had to know the word."

She did not discuss any recollections of writing at school. However, she did mention her performance in and her perception of school plays: "For example, in the fifth and sixth grade, the teachers picked out all the smart kids who could memorize a sheet and put them in a play. The teachers never thought that I could participate in a play." However, Ella "squeezed in there anyway in the seventh grade," noting that she "got on stage" by repeatedly telling the teacher that she "*could do it*." The seventh-grade teacher who believed in her and gave her a part in the play was the teacher who also thought Ella "was going to be somebody." By contrast, in church, she had been encouraged to perform in plays every Christmas and Easter for years. Although the elementary school population was still somewhat homogeneous, school was a place where children were grouped according to teachers' perceptions. Reading, memorizing, and speaking properly were valued capital, but as a seventh grader, Ella was willing to fight to prove to her teachers that she "*could do it*," She was still willing to fight perceptions and not shut down.

During high school desegregation, Ella feared "being killed or shot," ideas, she said, "which went through my mind for awhile." Although this danger never became reality, an observable distance from the white students prevailed: "The white kids would sit on one side of the classroom, and we'd sit on the other side. They didn't want anything to do with us. And when the bell rang, they went down one side of the hallway, and we went down the other. Teachers didn't want us in the classrooms. The white kids would sit on one side and open up the windows—like they were afraid to breathe the same air we breathed."

Ella observed literacy among the white students in this new environment: "On the bus a third-grade white kid would be reading a book we'd read in the eighth grade, and my mouth would fly open! And I would say, '*We are doomed*.' But I hung in there; I didn't do my best, but I didn't fit in with the white kids. They would recite and read, and I'd get real nervous." She did read *To Kill a Mockingbird* and *Lord of the Flies* and, during the interview, she recalled specifics of each book and discussed them with me. Continuing her comments about being in school with the white kids, she said, "I tried to make it, but the time wasn't right. I felt like I was too old to fix; my ways were set in. The level I was taught on, when I went to the white school, I felt like I had to jump levels—to advance. I didn't talk. I didn't want to admit it. Some went on, some. I remember two white teachers—thought all blacks looked alike. My white home ec teacher, though—sweet, loved me, helped me. One day she told me to make a pound cake. *Left me alone, in charge.* When she came back, she ate that cake and gave me a B and told me it was good even though it wasn't."

In third grade, her loving and gentle teacher had kept Ella after school to help her with her reading. She had encouraged her with powerful words. In seventh grade, Ella's teacher gave her a part in a play and believed that she could do it. But in high school, Ella had to use literacy properly in front of white teachers and students, whom she sensed did not want her there, whom she sensed could not *see* her. Ella knew she had not read the same books as the white children; the third grader had taught her a frightening lesson about the used textbooks she had been reading for years. Now race and class combined as powerful factors to shut Ella out of educational success and the cultural trappings that accompanied it, and Ella decided to shut down: Her "ways were set in," and as a teenager, she believed she was "too old to fix." The same Ella who had been told that she "was going to be somebody."

Her own awareness of economic, educational, and racial distance at a critical point in her life made her *feel* that she wasn't "college material"—exactly the same comment made about her daughter, who is now a college graduate. She noted, "I am so proud of my kids because they are getting what I didn't get." She commented on their textbooks and their "essays," but she expressed frustration because she does not believe that she can help them with their homework.

Ella overcomes her insecurities and desire to shut down for her children. She goes to school for conferences about her children's work, and she recalled one group of teachers: "The instant I met them, I felt as though they were looking at me like a let-down. They probably picked up on my accent, probably said I wasn't anything. And therefore, when they *picked this up from me*, they probably would say that my child wouldn't be anything either." In this situation, Ella again perceived herself as distanced educationally and socioeconomically from those in power, and she also *believed* that her child would be distanced or shut out of school life because of her educational and class status. I asked her about the racial composition of the group of teachers, and she said that the teachers in this group were both African American and white.

After this meeting, she put her child in another school. Again, she met with teachers, but this time she went "well dressed, hair in place, jewelry, heels"—dressed "properly" for this institution, but still wearing her life experiences. Ella told the teachers that she needed help with English and mathematics and that she did not want her child "stigmatized because of [her]." The teachers were supportive, and they offered to help her child, who did well academically in this setting.

Ella understands school success and all that influences it: race, correct speech, dress, and literacy capital. In fighting for her children's right to an education, she has refused to shut down. She knows that she must "voice her opinion" even if she may sense that she is being perceived arrogantly. But Ella's early lessons about herself and her background were so powerful that she has never learned to be totally comfortable with who she is and where she is from. Fortunately, several people helped her internalize that she should be proud of who she is—a talented, articulate, and compassionate woman who fights for her children and her beliefs.

Julia's Story

As a young girl, Julia believed, "God was getting me ready for the world." She used to daydream that she was riding in a convertible in New York. She had never been to New York, but she knew that she was "trying to get there"; her daydreams told her that someday she would leave home.

Julia, an African American woman in her forties, described growing up in the rural South: "It was a small community....We lived from the land. When you learned to walk, you had a job. You were told one time what to do, and you did that for the rest of your days, *as long as you were home*. We worked in the fields all day long." Julia and her family picked cotton, beans, and peas, and Julia "hated it." She added, "There was no word of being tired in your vocabulary; you just knew what you had to do. Financially, we were very poor people, but we lived off the land, and we had a comfortable life. Because anything that could be grown, we grew it. And even though we grew it, we would go into the fields and pick the leftovers—*and I might as well say it*—

after the white people had picked what they wanted. But we always had; we never went hungry."

In this early interview, Julia overcame a momentary hesitance to describe the hierarchy of whites and African Americans in the rural South when she was growing up. Race was a factor in our interview process, as it had been with Ella when she referred to the need of white people to get rid of old books; for example, white people, in our initial interview became "they." Julia, Ella, and I had grown up in similar rural areas in the South during the same time period, but we had all learned racial and social separation rather than connection while growing up. We had been taught to distance ourselves from people in other racial groups, and now in our conversations that need to distance ourselves had to be overcome by "naming." Neither Ella nor Julia shut down when recalling racial inequalities or injustice in my presence, and I urged them to speak.

Growing up, Julia attended church every Sunday whether she was sick or not. She was told that it was the right place to be, and the church was her life, in many ways. Her job each week was to "jump up and ring the church bell" to tell others to come. Church impressed her. She saw and heard the sisters shout, and she "heard the words" of the preacher. While Julia did not read and write in this small church, she heard and internalized the words spoken and sung. As she grew older, she worked with the little children, and she was always in the choir. As with Ella, church for Julia was a safe house.

In her church now, which is largely African American, Julia is frequently called on to sing. "I'm a listening ear," she said, "and I don't want to voice my opinion, but I will give you a song. And it's not that I'm stealing the show, but this is the only way I know how to give someone else my *world of knowledge*." She closes her eyes during these performances, because she neither wants nor needs to see faces or reactions. She learned as a child that singing in church is a way to express emotions and feelings and that the church is a safe place for this kind of expression by a woman. Julia has found that one's *world of knowledge* can be communicated creatively if other means of communication are blocked.

Julia had no idea of the educational level of her family members. She remembered few books in her childhood home: "a Bible and a set of encyclopedias that I didn't know how to deal with." She had no memories of being read to as a child. Julia had beautiful handwriting, though, and her female cousin frequently asked Julia to write letters for her. She admired Julia's handwriting, and she "read" the letters. Julia thus learned that her writing had the potential to win praise and admiration and that it could be used to communicate.

Julia had "no self-esteem." She was picked on mercilessly by her classmates in school. She recalled that males often "compared" her to other females and called her names. She stated, "I was made to look down on myself at an early age, and I was stripped of my self-esteem, of any confidence in believing in myself." During this time and in this place, at home and at school, she said *You weren't allowed to speak; you listened. You heard. So whatever you thought or whatever your feelings were, you didn't know you had any. You did what you were told to do. You couldn't speak; your opinion didn't mean anything.*"

Julia's responses to questions about school literacy were silence. The topic of school created a shutdown in her, one which I have chosen to respect. She had no memories that she wished to share, other than the fact that she was "one of the most picked on children" in school. From the first grade through her elementary school years, she was beaten by kids every day; her "head was beaten raw." She recalled derogatory comments about her appearance made even by the male principal. She felt shut out of school; being a female in an institution headed by a male who allowed and even contributed to this degradation, she could never find a positive sense of identity.

When asked about reading at school, Julia responded quickly that she "always avoided it and got away with it." When asked if she recalled any embarrassing moments reading at school, she laughed knowingly and stated that she never had any, because she avoided the act of reading. She learned to distance herself from any embarrassing moments by choosing not to read. Sardonically reeling off the words, Julia stated that reading at school started with "Jack and Jill went up the hill/ To fetch a pail of water," and then stated she had no memories of reading after that. Julia also avoided writing at school because she was afraid of making mistakes and, because she assumed that she would be scolded, she just did not do it at all. Interestingly, Julia is a highly intelligent woman who learned to read and write quite well. She obviously chose not to share her abilities with anyone at school for fear of failure or punishment. Brandt's (1990) description of school as a "house of language-on-its-own" is applicable; school was neither a safe house for Julia nor was it an important house, for reading and writing done there served only as more opportunities for embarrassment and ridicule. She discovered her own purposes for these acts later. Julia's clipped responses, her cynical laughter, her perfectly patient pauses for my next questions revealed a deadening shutdown occurring at school early in Julia's life, an institution that again would fail her in adulthood after a life-threatening illness.

In her teens, she escaped the hard work of country life and fled to the large city where she now resides. Like Ella, she was chided because of where she was from. She stated: "When I *grew up* and *grew out* of that area and moved away from it, city people made me feel *inferior*. I wouldn't tell anybody where I was from"; she did this in order to prevent ridicule and to distance herself from her rural background. She also learned that a certain vocabulary was dangerous; it might reveal who you were and where you were from. In the city, she was chided about believing in "voodoo and roots," and, although she "was not raised like that," she fought arrogant perceptions such as these about rural southern life. In the city she graduated from high school with good grades, had several jobs, and then got married and got pregnant. After that, she became seriously ill; in fact, it was a miracle that she recovered. She and her husband divorced, and she reared her children. After her illness, not only did she support them, she also taught herself to write and forced herself to walk again, and she is now employed. Julia is a quiet fighter, a woman of incredible perseverance.

Her descriptions of herself are humble. They reveal a private woman who stays to herself: "a quiet person, a background person, a behind-the-door person." Julia says that she belongs to God, that she is God's child—a woman who, like the grandparents who raised her, is not a complainer. Rather, she can deal with all of life's circumstances and people from all walks of life as she acts as God's servant to others. She attributes her education to "*wisdom, God's wisdom*," not to teachers or to schools. It is the oral lessons she learned in her childhood church that are at odds with literate practice in late 20th century America. "If we are all God's children," she asks, "why do some people think they are better than others?" And why do those who think they are better use "forms," printed documentation, and "piles of paper" to define and categorize people who have less than themselves?

Her current home is filled with pictures, books, magazines, and newspapers. She reads the Bible, *Ebony*, *Jet*, *Southern Living*, and *McCall's*, as well as local newspapers. It is writing, however, on which she relied to make herself "heard" after her medical recovery— writing that she remembered pleasantly. After her illness, she knew that in order to take care of herself and her children, she would have to learn to write with her left hand; speech was impossible in the early stages of recovery. She was literally denied her voice for a period of time. "I wanted to talk, but I could only sit and *write* my feelings," she explained. She kept telling herself that she "had to learn to write all over again" in order to gain independence and maintain privacy. "I wrote the things that I felt—things that had been so wrapped up in me, things that had just lain there dormant inside."

As an African American female in the rural South, she had been taught not to speak, not to voice her opinions. As a child, she had found herself subject to males and wealthier whites. Her situation, too, was what Stanback (1988) described as a "triple jeopardy" situation. She recalled, however, that her cousin had admired her writing; writing was her only way to be heard, and as an adult, she fought to use it. She could "speak" safely, maybe even elicit praise, without saying a word. While her children were at school, she "wrote and wrote and wrote" and then would sit back and read her own words. Julia created a reflective tool, a way to have dialogue with herself through a medium that she remembered positively from her childhood encounters with her encouraging cousin.

At our first meeting, she shared with me a manuscript, enclosed in a protective folder, which she had written during this time in her life. It is an important document reflecting her thoughts, her struggles, and her courage finally in finding a way to speak and to be heard. Julia also writes poetry to "relieve the emotion of a situation" and often puts the words to music. She has found her own use for writing —a far cry from the writing sanctioned as correct by many schools.

Julia eventually believed that she could go back to work, and one of the important moments that stood out in her mind was when she tried to get someone to provide "signature support," a letter of reference, for a job for which she was applying. She recalled that no one wanted to support her with a "signature." However, she was hired finally by a woman who handed Julia her time sheet, a piece of paper, and a pencil and then said, "Now—you do it. You *can* do it." Julia remembered the encounter with this woman—how it affected her life and her self-concept. She recalled the "nice" sound of her boss's voice as she spoke and her attitude towards Julia in the workplace. Julia responded, "I did do it. And I felt so good about myself. You see, she believed in me when I didn't believe in myself, and she trusted me. She didn't treat me as though she was one step above me—as though I was *nobody*. She worked *with* me. All I had felt was that I was a failure, but she had hope in me. She knew what I could do. I had always been afraid of making a mistake, but she continued to tell me in a *very gentle way that I could do it. She had faith in me.*" The woman who hired Julia was a white woman, a college graduate, but she was as Julia stated, "a Christian" who had no arrogant perceptions about being better than Julia.

In order to get help with learning to write again, Julia tried to enroll in an adult education writing class. She was never accepted, and she believes this was due to her age and to not knowing the right person—"someone who could recommend me or put me into that school." Although she taught herself, she stated that she "was hurt," for she loved to write. If she did not "feel comfortable talking to someone," she knew that she could sit down and write, "just write." Julia perceived the institution of school, from her segregated elementary school to an integrated and diverse adult education program, as a place focusing on comparisons, failure, embarrassment, and "better-than-you" people. Fortunately, in the workplace she found an encouraging mentor who had high expectations for her and treated her with respect and dignity. This mentor genuinely invited Julia into another world, and Julia gladly went.

During one of our interviews, Julia, shared her frustration about government agencies and their use of literacy: their "*piles of paper*" and their "*terminology.*" She described a frustrating meeting that she had attended when those in charge referred to those receiving governmental assistance as "cases"—their lives "all piled up in folders" and tossed into bins if they were deemed unworthy of assistance. Julia had been "invited" to attend these meetings and share her feelings about possible improvements that could be made in service delivery.

Julia, however, soon sensed that those receiving assistance were perceived by those in charge as not worthy of respect. She closed her eyes and passionately said that she told herself: "No more, no more. And—I just—*shut down*. That's what I did because I felt so used. There are days that I *shut down*. Just like a light switch. I say, 'Okay, switch. I'm cutting you off.'" She excused herself from the meeting by saying that she was going to the restroom, but she fled the building and returned safely to her home. She laughed and said, "I went to the restroom at my house."

I asked about the people who worked in these agencies—actually, it turned out, people a lot like myself. Julia answered, "Bigwigs, Ph.D.s. Big people, dripping in jewelry, big diamonds, big cars." Teachers, social workers, governmental bureaucrats; people like myself, I realized, as Julia talked on.

She then described the meetings prior to her final shutdown and restroom exit. She entered "a nicely lit conference room" and found her name on a card on a table. She said, "I was expecting a senator or somebody important to walk through the door any minute. I felt special." But, she soon noted that the meetings went "as *they* wanted." After one of the meetings, she read a newspaper article about the meetings. She said, "I started reading, and I started reading *my own words*, and then the article said who said those words—that a man said them. *But I said those words. I was so hurt.* He was a man in power, but he had no knowledge. I began to feel that I was being used to do their job." She was never mentioned in any articles about the meetings, and no quotes were attributed to her. Yet at the meetings, those in charge encouraged those invited to speak.

At one meeting, she recalled, in order to keep people focused in their discussion, the meeting facilitators used a grouping technique during which topics of "relevance" to *their* interests were listed on large pieces of poster board and taped to the walls. Topics mentioned, but not believed to be of "primary importance," were listed on designated poster boards called "parking lots." These topics were "parked," to be discussed if there was time. Julia remarked, "Only important issues that *they wanted to talk about* could be worked on." Although Julia had been invited to participate in civic dialogue that presumably involved decision making, this rhetorical practice of privileging topics quickly shut her out from those in power.

She learned that her fate was in the hands of those she described as "big people." She remarked that these people had the power to give her "the boldness" she so desperately wanted—if only they had acknowledged her opinions and respected her as a person. Julia explained further, *"There was—no God in them. At first I felt honored, good to be chosen, but then it was like I was being raped. And they didn't see any hurt because their minds were focused on so many other things."*

Julia was willing to enter another world and risk being shut out. She is a fighter, a woman who has hope. All she needed was an invitation. But she shut down once again and was given neither respect nor credit for her ideas. Her ideas were appropriated by those in power, who seemed bound to their "piles of paper" and their "terminology," a legalistic and defining use of literacy in Julia's eyes; she sees all people as children of God, no one better than another. Writing, which Julia has found so liberating, also has the power to define people and reduce them and their lives to a folder to be read or one to be dismissed.

She concluded, "My advice to these people is to recognize God first in everything that they do, especially if they are helping God's people, and *we are his people*. But to keep looking out for their own bank accounts, their own paychecks, their living, they have got to walk over me to get where they are."

Beverly's Story

During my first meeting with Beverly, she told me about "her new life." Her husband had retired recently from a demanding job that had "dictated her life." Before his retirement, she had felt compelled to associate with his subordinates and their wives at social functions, and she believed that she played a role in his career advancement. She stated emphatically, "I have performed properly, entertained nicely, and been a role model to the families of the people who worked for my husband." But she confessed that she had "hated" to go to social functions with them. She had felt obligated to appear "respectable" and, in retrospect, she did not believe that she "tried to mix very well." In fact, she had distanced herself from them as much as possible.

Beverly also described herself as a "background, behind-the-scenes person," a person who "does not like to stand out," and the visibility she experienced with her husband's role as a corporate official discomforted her. Her expected behavior was "made real" with the help of literacy in company protocol guidelines, which she likened to a "book on how to behave." In many ways, she wanted "to be one of the group" and not "to appear any better than any of the wives whose husbands worked for her husband." Beverly stated, "I wanted to be accepted on their level, but I—I wanted to—it sounds very snooty—but I wanted to stoop down a bit, didn't want to appear any better than any of them. Because I wasn't. However, uhhhh—I was."

I queried, "What—made you—feel better, superior to them?"

Beverly pondered, "I think it's ingrained."

We pushed on. In our conversations, she verbalized, after much probing, the sources of her discomfort with those who worked "for her husband" and of her need to create distance between them and herself. She admitted that she had perceived that her own family had "higher standards": "a better house, more money, different language usage, more and finer material possessions (clothes, furniture), education—*our way of doing things, our background, our upbringing.*" Upon reflecting on this part of the interview and examining the words on the transcripts, Beverly was quite moved and upset by her admissions.

Repeatedly, she stated, *"This is terrible. I can't believe that this is how I feel. I never—never—was so shocked at myself. I didn't know I had these thoughts."* These feelings, as time went on, proved to be examples of a learned arrogance and justification for shutting people out of her world.

She revealed that during the research period, she urged her husband to read her transcripts. She reported to me that he was shocked to learn that she had hated these social events. He was unaware of her true feelings, and she admitted that during her marriage she had silenced her feelings because she did not want to create an unpleasant situation. She added, "He never knew my true feelings, and I never communicated them to him." But since his retirement, she believes that this has changed.

Beverly's attitudes about background seemed to be learned, in various and intersecting ways, through three institutions in her life: her family of origin, her schooling, and her husband's business. The beliefs transmitted to Beverly about social status for most of her life have been at odds with her caring personality and religious beliefs. The beliefs transmitted through her church were in conflict with any kind of superiority over others. To her childhood church, which she attended only with her mother, she attributed her learning "to love and to care for others" and, since her husband's retirement, Beverly has made the church the focus of her new life.

Realizing that she had experienced a strong sense of dissonance during her husband's career, she wanted to discuss these issues matter-of-factly, and she in no way shut down any aspect of our conversation, for she repeatedly said that she wanted to learn and to grow—maybe as part of her "spiritual journey in her new life." In fact, she frequently called me with examples from her past involving what she and I termed "social distance"; she wanted to examine the experiences and understand them. She asked me to help her understand why she had distanced herself from people she perceived as different. She admitted that she had never really "known" many African Americans or many poor people; her circle of friends had always consisted of people with similar backgrounds to hers. According to Beverly, confidentiality, anonymity, and a common religious bond served to provide a safe house for our discussions.

When I asked her if she had ever known any black people, she responded that her family had "a couple of black people as hired help." Beverly then told me several stories. She had been troubled for some time that she "distanced" certain people, and she wanted to learn why. She stated that an African American woman had approached her once and confided to her that she felt that there were "barriers" in the group to which they both belonged. Beverly said, "I just dropped it. I cut her off." Beverly admitted that she simply did not know how to discuss racial barriers with this woman, so she just stopped the conversation. She was quite sincere concerning self-examination and growth. She displayed a great deal of courage in confronting some difficult issues with me, because she does find it difficult to talk about herself and her own life. Over the years, it has been ingrained in her to "perform properly" and not name her true feelings.

Beverly, a 60-year-old white woman, was born in a small northeastern U.S. town, and she lived in "one of the nicer houses" in her community. A "Yankee," she described her family as "well-to-do, never lacking for anything." Her father graduated from an Ivy League school. Her mother, too, was a college graduate and, although she never worked, she believed that she should have done something "more worthwhile with her life." Beverly simply stated, "It was an assumption that the children would all go to college. And it came easily—we did not have to work our way through—which is a disadvantage, in retrospect."

Telling her father, "the moneygiver," that she hated college, Beverly dropped out after her freshman year and went to secretarial school. She worked as a secretary for a short time; however, she found the work unchallenging, and she had little in common with her colleagues, whom she remembers as much older than she. Beverly stated, "In order to convince my father that I should be allowed to return to college and make something of my life, I had to agree to be tested for admission, and my father placed me in a small, New England type school." She completed her undergraduate degree and taught school for a few years.

Beverly described her family background, although affluent, as "miserable." In fact, she always tried to hide her father's educational level and occupation from new acquaintances, for she never wanted to feel "any better" than anyone else. She was quite aware that the family's affluence and educational background had the power to distance her from others, and she genuinely fought by concealment what might be perceived as appearing better than others.

Her parents divorced when she was young, and she has blocked many of her childhood memories. Her own marriage and family are central to her perceptions of accomplishment in life. She wished that her family of origin had been closer, and she has always been envious of families that have "big family reunions with T-shirts and picnics."

Beverly's childhood home had a den lined with shelves that were filled with books, magazines (including *Time*, which was a "good old Republican magazine at that time"), newspapers, encyclopedias, a Bible, and a series on Winston Churchill. Her father was a history buff; her mother, an avid reader. However, Beverly cannot remember being read to as a child. She just recalls that the books in her home were part of her family's background; they were visible background credentials, in essence. Beverly's home now is not filled with books; however, a few pretty books, one of which was a book of poems, graced the top of a chest. Beverly expressed a love of poems and stated that she understood that her great-grandmother and her mother felt the same way. The idea of loving poems has been transmitted generationally through the female lineage in the family, women whom Beverly remembered fondly.

Beverly reads diligently now, although it is not her favorite pastime. She reads magazines, including *Reader's Digest* because it is condensed, and *Guideposts*. She told me that she does not like to read "big books which are thick volumes or novels." However, during our discussion, she went to her bedroom to get some big books she is currently reading to show me that she does read them. She stated a love of biographies and autobiographies, books that show positive people overcoming challenges in their lives. She recommended Corrie Ten Boom's *The Hiding Place*, and she also showed me John Grisham's *The Rainmaker* and *The Firm* and Ronald Kessler's *Inside the White House*.

Although Beverly understands the importance of reading, for her it is "painful" for she reads word-for-word. She stated, "*I am not proud to say that I am not a reader. I get very embarrassed when people say, 'Have you read such and such?' or when they say, 'Let's form a book group.' I know that I could not participate. I just could not read fast enough, and I would feel terribly inadequate.*" Yet, Beverly could participate. She was quite excited showing me the books she had read, summarizing them, chatting about them. She simply does not read quickly, which always caused her embarrassment in school and with her father. This feeling of "*inadequacy*" affects her current reading practices.

Beverly also stated that she was not a writer and had no memories of anyone writing at home when she was growing up; however, she revealed that she now uses letter writing as a form of emotional expression. She described writing letters to her husband to vent her anger at him and then ripping up the letters. However, she immediately asked, "*Is that writing?*" She noted that frequently she found at a later time that she felt differently and that the letter writing provided a safe release of feelings, allowing for the avoidance of conflict. Her husband and her children have praised her letter-writing ability: her naturalness and her conversational tone in written format. Interestingly, one letter to a family member written during the research period created a family shutdown. Beverly's long overdue honesty was taken as an affront, and the recipient of the letter became angry. This anger was not what Beverly anticipated, and she was shocked at the letter's power to create this reaction. She used to keep a diary and is now keeping a journal; however, she stated, "I don't like things down in writing about myself." I asked her at this point why she had agreed to participate in this study, and she responded that at first she did not realize the interviews would be so "*in depth—having to review stuff about myself and talk back*." However, she was now confident that the research was anonymous and that she would learn about herself.

In fact, talking back was problematic for Beverly. At first, she wanted to give me correct responses; she was not completely comfortable with my probing. She also wanted me to behave as a researcher and just ask the questions and get the responses. The reflection required by both of us was unnerving to her at first. She wanted me to be professional by distancing myself from the research data instead of questioning my own distancing from some aspects of it. To her credit, she had no trouble telling me how she felt. She is an honest woman who is determined to learn and grow.

Growing up, piano and dance recitals were an integral part of Beverly's life. She loved piano so much that when she played school as a child she was a music teacher. She recalled her first and last dance recital, the culmination of her mother's attempt to make her graceful: "I didn't like performing because I was in the foreground, but I found myself in the back row for the first recital because I wasn't good enough." She fell during the performance and, although her mother praised her, "that was the end of ballet." Not performing properly necessitated a shutdown from this type of performance, which was subject to perfection and the approval of parents and their friends.

Much like Ella, Beverly openly shared in the early part of our first interview some of her thoughts that might cause her to distance herself from me: "I will be very self-conscious because I know you are an expert in *grammar*." She said that she believed that she was "weak in grammar," and at that point shared stories of a close female friend who frequently corrected her grammar while they were shopping. Over time, the friend's corrections made Beverly feel "*terribly self-conscious and ill at ease*" in her presence. Beverly continued this relationship, but she shut down certain aspects of conversation, which might be subject to correction, and simply internalized her frustration at being corrected in social settings. She chose to be silenced rather than possibly make a grammatical error in speech or confront the woman with her feelings.

While Beverly is aware of how it feels to have one's speech and usage corrected by others, she readily shared that her grandmother disapproved of Beverly's husband because "his family was blue collar." She recalled her own feelings: "*His family was honorable and loving, but, indeed, their background and grammar were noticeable.*" She went on to explain that her husband's parents had unfortunate backgrounds and that neither had graduated from college. She added, "*There was a lot of ain't's, a lot of cussing, and the grammar was very noticeable.*" But Beverly defied her grandmother and married her husband. At that young age, she admitted that she "had no idea of the importance of backgrounds," but she now believes that they are important and that they include "one's education, one's economic level, one's way of doing things, and one's upbringing."

After recalling the episodes with her friend who silenced her by correcting Beverly's grammar and after recalling her grandmother's arrogant attitude toward Beverly's husband's parents, she asked me about another situation. She admitted—even as we were discussing these issues and she was consciously upset by her admissions—that she was currently bothered by a friend who "has pronunciation problems." At my prompting, Beverly listed some of them: "bof" for *both*, "birfday" for *birthday*, "carrying" someone to the store. She stated that these "problems" were "*very noticeable when the person comes into our circle of friends.*" Beverly reflected and responded honestly as usual, "*This person is not educated, only a high school graduate, who lives in a rural southern community.*"

Growing up, Beverly attended her mother's church for about 15 years; her father, she recalled, would have nothing to do with her mother's religion, which Beverly described laughingly as a "wacko religion." She said that as a child she felt connected and secure in this church composed of people who "tended to have money," for she was "darling little Beverly, her mother's daughter"; however, she felt "embarrassment" telling anyone outside this group which church she attended. She recalled reading "little scriptures" in this church and hearing powerful testimonies, personal stories of miracles. She remembers this church fondly, though, for it was a "safe, happy place" filled with "very loving, caring, and positive people." The members of this church loved her mother, and Beverly stated, "It was good to see her loved." Beverly credits this church and her "positive and considerate" mother for her own need for a caring church and for her desire "to reach out to those in need."

She is active in her current church, a mainstream Protestant church; in fact, she commented, *"This church is an integral part of me. It is safe, warm, and loving. And it's a newfound thing for me at this point in my life, now that I am more free; this church provides a venue to help people in their life crises, and I never realized how important it is for me to help others."* Beverly serves on committees and sings in the choir for which she "didn't have to try out." In this place, she was accepted readily. She enjoys the "real messages" conveyed through music, and she also admitted that by being in the choir, she did not feel compelled to teach Sunday school, where she would feel inadequate because of her lack of Biblical knowledge. The inadequacy again would stem from the need to read in order to prepare lessons. Like Ella and Julia, Beverly finds through church musical programs a safe place for expression and nonthreatening, noncompetitive performance.

Even though Beverly's own religious faith is dear to her, she still feels slightly uncomfortable discussing religious matters openly. She shared a strong reaction she had to a Christmas letter she had received from friends, who described their new religion and shared their spiritual experiences. Beverly did not read these paragraphs, skipping over them and shutting out the written efforts to communicate with her, because she felt their words were "out of place."

Beverly perceived her own religion as a child as "wacko," and she did not want others to know of her participation in it. In fact, she stated that this religion may have been a contributing factor to her parents' divorce. Although Beverly uses letter writing to express her emotions, expressing one's religious beliefs so openly is uncomfortable to her. Beverly knows that discussing religious beliefs is not always safe; it can lead to conflict. She added as she continued to reflect, "I do not like to wear religion on my sleeve and stand out in any way."

Beverly's discussion of reading at school began with the private kindergarten, owned by a family friend, which she attended. Attending this school was a "status symbol," and Beverly's siblings went there, also. She noted, "I apparently did well enough that the teacher advanced me into the second grade." She never went to first grade, and she "never learned how to read *properly*." She attributes this problem to not getting "the basics, such as phonics," and she "believes that [she] must have done something wrong in kindergarten." Throughout school, she felt as though she were a "year behind" and that "reading was always a problem." In fact, at this point in the interview, she described herself as a "nonreader," one whom her father eventually "shipped out of public school to another private school" during her high school years. She stated, "My father, who was not conscious of my school work and who did not live with me, insisted on this change because the private school to which I was sent offered remedial reading." She remarked, "The school didn't help much; I just had a ball there."

Beverly, who reads word-for-word, "faked" reading aloud. It was silent reading and timed reading that plagued her, but somehow she "muddled through it." She stated that if we were simultaneously reading silently the same passage, she would "just kind of skim down and finish before" me, and "not know one word that was on the page." She admitted she has done this all of her life, for she "is a slow reader who reads every word, who is not comfortable—*skipping any words*!" She added, "I feel like I've missed a lot; there is so much to offer in books, but I have *no skimming tools*."

Reading and corresponding writing assignments in high school were "dreaded, horrible" occasions, although writing itself was "never difficult." Beverly took any shortcut in order to "abbreviate reading, so the pain would be less." Book reports were memorable to her; she chose to report on books about which movies had been made—"any shortcut possible." The books she was compelled to read in school never interested her. She continuously checked the "bottom of the pages to see how many pages had been read—and the clock." She noted, "*I would say, 'Oh, my gosh. I've only read x amount in half an hour.'*" So when given the choice, she "looked for skinny books."

As an adult, Beverly loved teaching reading to young children. When I asked her how she approached the teaching of reading, she said, "It was a chore getting the fundamentals and the basics; phonics is not the most exciting thing. But I *emphasized* reading to them. We went to the library every 2 weeks, and I would get at least 30 books—on their grade level—for their library corner. I picked out neat stories to read to them at the end of the day, and nobody slept. I *wanted* them to be interested in books." Beverly did not avoid reading as a teacher; she did not shut down. She wanted for her students what she herself did not have.

She recalled writing more in college than in high school; her high school English teachers were "not strong, just average." She noted, "Writing was never difficult—if I had command of the situation and was allowed to select my own subject." But most writing in school was actually "a chore," because it had to have "sources." What she remembered about writing in school was "mechanics and books on how to write papers."

As we have seen in her adult life, Beverly has used writing to express pent-up emotion and to connect or disconnect with others safely, without having to move into the "foreground" of conflict and without face-to-face contact. In addition to letter writing, she keeps a journal, and as it is for Julia and Ella, writing is a way to speak and to make one's thoughts known safely.

Writing is a way to express what she feels, but even writing is dictated by what is perceived to be correct, as are speaking and reading. Ella perceived certain people as correct; in fact, she stated that I was correct. Beverly has spent most of her life trying to be correct by performing properly. She was expected to attend certain schools and go to college. She was expected to associate with people who had a certain background—a background linked to their educational and economic level, their manner of speaking, and their grammar. She was expected to read in a certain way, at a certain rate, and not to reveal that she did not or could not read in this manner. Exercising his power over her, her father "shipped" her to a private school to attempt to fix her reading inadequacy.

Beverly herself admitted to shutting down others. When faced with reading her friends' letter that revealed "out of place" topics, she chose to distance herself by not reading it. When faced with discussing racial barriers, she "cut the person off." Beverly, much like the teachers in Brodkey's (1990) study, often has chosen to alienate and distance herself when confronted with "class concerns."

As Beverly illustrates, Ella did not imagine perceived *correctness and being shut out*. After hearing Beverly describe the person whose pronunciation disturbed her, I became sure that Ella was correct in saying that she is sometimes judged on being from the rural South, on speaking with an accent featuring certain dialectal patterns, and on being "just" a high school graduate. Learned arrogance is real: It is transmitted by family members, by teachers, and by those at the top of the ladder of American success; it is transmitted by our material wealth; it is transmitted by the exclusionary circles we create. It ripples into literacy use and has consequences for literacy practices. As it affects one's perceptions of correct reading, writing, and speaking, learned arrogance is a force powerful enough to keep some people out of certain circles perceived to be more correct than others. For those safely within correct circles, it is a force powerful enough to keep them from using literacy tools; they might slip up and reveal what they have been taught to believe is an inadequacy in themselves.

Sarah's Story

Born in the South, Sarah told me that she grew up in an "industrial area—but not in an area of coal mines or poverty." Groping for the right words, Sarah, a white woman in her forties, finally stated that her family lived in a "rather affluent, middle- or upper-middle-class neighborhood." She remembered them living at first in a "nice, cozy, small house" and soon moving to a larger house that she described as "cold, distant, and sterile." Her very strict parents came from poor backgrounds but, "as time went on, they just moved up the ladder." She described her parents as "highly intelligent, very educated, knowledgeable about everything." Her father had a college degree; her mother, 2 years of college. Sarah did not recall "talking" to her mother; rather, she recalled "battling" with her. Her mother was a strict disciplinarian who often "smacked" her children. When Sarah's father came home from work, he disciplined by talking to the children, which seemed to hurt Sarah more than being spanked. Even in high school, Sarah's mother still selected Sarah's clothes, clothes she deemed appropriate. Sarah, who was not allowed to try out for cheerleading, was not allowed to make choices for herself because she might make inappropriate choices.

She interjected at a later point in our interviews:

"It's funny. If you had asked me when I was growing up about my family, I would have said that we were dirt poor because even though we lived in a fine house with everything we needed, that is how I perceived it. It was just one of those unspoken things, that from day one, I was led to believe that we didn't have any money; it was really a strong feeling, that even though we lived in a nice house, we were very poor. I remember when Barbies came out and, for my birthday, instead of getting me a *real Barbie*, Mom and Dad got me a *knock-off Babette*. And that was the way everything was. It wasn't that we didn't have money; they just always bought me something to substitute for the *real thing*. And it's probably that they grew up in the Depression era. They were always careful with their money, I guess. Mom and Dad told stories about orange crate furniture and homemade clothes. It was just part of the way they approached life. If there had been *Calvin Klein* jeans, I would have had *J.C. Penney* jeans."

Literacy used by advertisers and businesses helped to create "real things" in Sarah's mind. This use of literacy and symbols allowed Sarah to distinguish between those who possessed "real things" and those who did not. It also fueled an ongoing internal tug-of-war between a Sarah, who wanted to be herself and the culturally perfect person others expected her to be.

When asked about the impact of the Depression stories, she stated that the stories did not affect her as much as her parents' repeated actions—actions they justified through their stories. Sarah *never felt* as though she had the "better-than-you" things mentioned by Ella, and she never felt as though she fit in, yet she wanted to badly. "In order not to feel inferior or like a square peg in a round hole," she said, "I spent most of my life trying to become everything to everybody and to be what people—parents, teachers, and church friends—*expected*. I tried to make sure that I was what they wanted so that they would like me."

Sarah commented on these three areas of her life—home, public school, and the church—as powerful influences in her life: "They were all very rigid and very structured. Not very much fun—everything had to be done *exactly* to the model, no freedom, *rote memorization*. My early models in *how to live life* gave me the impression that there was one way to do things, only one way, and that things had to be done *perfectly*, that *rigidity* was the way things had to be accomplished. Because these institutions were so rigid and so structured, books were the freedom that was outside the structure. My mind could enter into the books, and that's why I read a lot of fantasy and a lot of stories about people doing things outside my *experience*."

Early in life when she did not feel accepted for herself or when she was not praised for attempts at self-expression, she "felt like crawling in a hole and became very quiet and isolated." In her isolation, however, she could at least read freely the thoughts created by authors in their books. As she shut down in some respects, books offered her mental escape routes.

Describing her adult life, Sarah said that she had completed 2 years of college and "a lot of living." She noted that her husband works for a major company and "has quite a title." She has had a variety of jobs, but none have required writing, which she strongly resists. Currently, she does not work. She believes that "God has richly provided us with more than enough to live comfortably and to have everything we need."

Sarah stated that she now is looking at life in new ways; previously she would have described herself as having "no self-esteem, struggling, not happy, a shell walking around doing what [she] had to do day-by-day." Now, however, she seeks friendships in support groups and through her church where she has finally met people "who seem to be who they really are and okay with that, healthy people who don't have to pretend to be other than who they are." By her own description, she is "a work-in-progress" and learning to be more comfortable with herself. Today, she flees "rigid people and programs," and she perceives the current church of which she is part as an accepting and tolerant institution.

Like Beverly, Sarah's childhood home was filled with books: "a lot of textbooks, *knowledge* books, two sets of encyclopedias, and one set of Childcraft [books]." She recalled that her parents' college textbooks lined the shelves—visible symbols of their educational level. Little Golden Books and other children's books were always available to the children in the family. Books became for Sarah an "endless source of knowledge and a means of escape."

When Sarah was in elementary school, the local library sponsored reading contests. Sarah filled out pages, got stickers, and won awards—always "excelling." Reading more pages than anyone else, she usually "came up first or second place in the whole town." She motivated herself to participate because this was an activity that she enjoyed. However, at home, Sarah recalled, "When I was a *bad* person or out of control with my temper, I was *sentenced* to my room, which was fine with me because I read and fantasized there. Reading was just a way of dealing with uncomfortable situations."

In her adult life, she continues to read extensively. She enjoys science fiction and mysteries. She recalled, "Several years ago my own child recognized that I had to be careful when reading because I could not read Stephen King, for example. I became too enmeshed with the characters, the plot. King is too dark." Sarah continued, "I take on a different personality, so I must recognize that this reading is escapism for me."

Sarah recalled writing "poems and little short stories—just little scribbles" when she was young. She did not share her little scribbles, but she did dare to share a few poems with her parents. However, even as a child she did not get the response she was looking for. She wanted a certain response: "Praise—adulation—What a good job!—or This should be published!" Laughing, she noted that instead she got, "'Well ... that's nice,' and then I stopped showing them my poems because I did not have a high tolerance for emotional pain." She explained, "When I didn't get the response I was looking for, I felt *shutdown, and I don't go back there. And the safe areas got fewer and fewer as time went on.*" Julia got praise for writing as a child and, in her later life, it became an escape route. Sarah, however, learned as a child that her writing did not elicit praise, and she avoids it to this day.

"Dodging and refusing" jobs that have required writing skills, Sarah dislikes writing intensely, for to her it is not a safe form of expression. However, she goes into the experiences and worlds of fictional others, safely through reading. Writing demands revealing self and allowing others into her private world, and she therefore exercises a high level of avoidance. She fears that her faults will be "recorded and permanent." She noted that her writing would have to be "censored," filled with "cross-outs, white-out, red ink, and the spelling would have to be right." However, she argued with me and with herself that she reads "enough to know that writers don't always follow rules." Sarah fears that someone might not like the Sarah revealed on paper—a "real" Sarah, one not constructed by advertisers and middle-class cultural expectations, so she takes no risks of revealing an "imperfect" person. She is currently "committed to keeping a daily journal, a very limited journal"; the space on which to write—Sarah measured it—is about four inches per day. The space is so confined that Sarah said, "I can bring myself to say and put down what I need to say in just a few words." She even selects greeting cards that have little blank space, just enough for her signature.

Sarah did recall her grandparents encouraging her in performance at home. At an early age, she remembered being "a real ham and *wanting* to dance and twirl and sing—just to be the center of attention and the main attraction of the stage." Her mother and father were always too busy to watch and to give any praise; as Sarah put it, "They didn't have time to sit down and watch some little moppet going through all kinds of shenanigans."

Those powerful influences—home, church, and school—were, indeed, "rigid and structured." They seemed, according to Sarah's descriptions and perceptions, to be filled with busy people intent on shaping perfect people through the transmission of knowledge and rules to which one should adhere. Knowledge in these institutions was transmitted within strong, sharply defined boundaries resulting in few options for those teaching or learning. Sarah's only safe means for crossing the boundaries were through reading books; if she had written honestly, she would have wanted to think outside these boundaries, to explore and express opinions, and someone in power might have seen an "incorrect" Sarah. She also may have misspelled a word.

Music also might have been a means for expression, for Sarah began playing a band instrument in elementary school and became quite accomplished. However, her playing frustrated her because this learned rigidity transferred into the world of music. Consequently, to this day she can play only what is on the page. She anguished that she "cannot go outside and ad lib."

In all of Sarah's recollections, she is acutely aware of the powerful messages that shaped her. But it is her impressions of the institutions and people in them that are so indelibly etched in her mind. She looked at me and recalled, "I remember *exactly* the overall tone and feeling of the teachers, the minister, the minister's wife, and my parents—and their words: *Thou shall not*—lots of them." She recalled "no affirmation, only guilt-production." For example, if she and her siblings did not sit still enough during the church service, they had to return home and spend 1 hour on the couch.

The members of Sarah's large city church were "moderately wealthy." She recalled that some people came "who were not well dressed, but that was the exception rather than the rule." I asked Sarah why she might recall a detail about church dress, and she explained that she had "a couple of friends from school who came [to church] from the wrong side of the tracks." Her town was segregated along racial and socioeconomic lines. Poor African Americans and whites tended to be segregated in one area of town, "and they rarely came out of that area to other social functions." She stated that "a few poor white kids" came to her church, probably because there was not a church in their area. Sarah did not really feel that she had many close friends at church; at retreats and meetings, the girls would form cliques, and she felt that she was always on the outside trying to fit in. In this description, Sarah recalled issues of class and the trappings of affluence. She had "friends" from "the wrong side of the tracks," and that was not acceptable to the girls who formed the church cliques; choosing inappropriate friends could exclude her from their circle.

In Sunday school, Sarah described the "standard little table with little chairs all around." Around this table, the children would take turns reading "*out loud*" from the "standard little lesson book." According to Sarah, "You stumbled over big words or whatever from the King James Version—a hard-to-digest text. You stumbled and felt like a fool. Again, I did not want to make a mistake in front of the long-suffering teacher and face the derision of the other kids." She recalled the New Testament stories as impressing her; on the other hand, the Old Testament stories were "*grim, judgmental, not filled with a lot of hope*." Sarah attributed her reaction to these stories to three factors: The Old Testament material was "dry"; the teachers did not seem to have a love for the material; and she did not interpret the material in a positive manner. Sarah recalled no writing in church. As is the case in many fundamentalist churches, writing (as expression or reflection) was not a pedagogical tool, for it might have allowed for questioning and debate (Zinsser, 1986), methods not tolerated by the rigid institutional framing (Bernstein, 1971).

She recalled being in church plays, and one memory, in particular, was pleasant. In this play, Sarah had few speaking lines; instead, she

59

danced. Her costume, she remembered, was "beautiful beyond description—gauzy and filmy"—and in part borrowed from a high school majorette. She was praised for her performance, and her response to praise and acceptance was strong. Smiling, she recalled that moment: *"That life was worth living; life was pretty good."*

Selecting a church has been a major decision each time Sarah and her husband have relocated. In her current struggle to find "healthy people and resist rigidity"—a resistance to shutting down— they now have found a church that is "comfortable." Sarah describes her current church as an accepting, nurturing, and encouraging institution. Here, she is "encouraged to do whatever." Involved in many activities and in many groups in this church, she has chosen roles that suit her. She is encouraged to read a wide range of Christian literature and to participate in discussions about her reading. She purposefully has chosen not to use her musical gifts in this church at this point, for she prefers to be in the "background" in her areas of service, because that is still the "safest."

Sarah's first memories of elementary school are pleasant. Surrounded by old trees, her elementary school was a "very old, three-story brick building which was like a maze with places to hide and let fantasy go." But then modernity and progress erased the familiar, as they had erased her "cozy" home, and she began her third grade year in a brand new *"too clean and too perfect and too sterile"* suburban school.

When she entered first grade, Sarah already knew how to read. She stated, "Once I figured out how to read, I read!" The already accomplished reader noted sarcastically that she had "fond" memories of learning the alphabet that year. But she recalled, "I hated to read aloud even though I read a lot." As in church, "anxiety would creep in," and she "stumbled over words," always afraid of not reading *"perfectly."* There were teachers in junior high and high school who "encouraged outside reading, things they considered age-appropriate and classic literature" over the summers. She recalled two English classes that focused "a whole unit on mythology and historical background," areas that fascinated her. But most of her school assignments did not challenge her and, to the displeasure of her parents and teachers, she refused to complete boring, rote assignments. She was often reprimanded and embarrassed for not reading what was assigned as homework, material she described as "never interesting, always factual and dry." Pondering for quite some time as to whether her school reading had influenced her reading habits and practices now, she finally concluded that although 12 years of exposure to books must have affected her in some way, her *love of reading and need for reading* were developed, ironically perhaps, during all of her "forced alone time." She resisted performing just for grades, her only means of rebellion. Had Sarah acquiesced to please her parents and teachers, she would have shut down.

Sarah described writing in school as "agony," and she attributed her hatred of writing specifically to her first- and fourth-grade teachers. Her fourth-grade teacher, "a real dragon of a teacher," used "a lot of red pencil and *sent* them [their compositions] back to us so we had to redo them—and that did not lead to *creativity*." Sarah never recalled writing creatively at school, but she did recall spelling when I asked about writing. She admitted,

> I am not a confident speller, and it's a thing that influences my writing. Before computer programs and spell-check, I would have to sit with a dictionary—right beside me—and it seems that I would even get stuck on the stupid, small words, something I just couldn't remember.

I asked Sarah to discuss how her teachers taught spelling, and she responded: "My teachers in the late 1950s and early 1960s made us spell by rote. Spelling phonetically had not been introduced or reintroduced. And memory is—memorizing things is a real problem to me. It may be a lack of discipline or concentration, but my mind takes off on flights of fancy, and I just do not think of myself as someone who needs to memorize things. So that was the problem. Spelling bees—I was always eliminated first or second round, and that was embarrassing. Spelling bees are fantastic for people who can memorize things or somehow read dictionaries and absorb spelling, but for people whose minds are not geared in that direction, they are terrible! What a demeaning, shaming game to introduce to people."

Spelling was not the only aspect of writing requiring memorization. Composing was not taught; instead Sarah learned to "just do" segmented aspects of writing by memorization: spelling, rules about sentence construction ("words *not* to have at the end of a sentence and dangling participles"), and "rules about how *it* [the paper] should go together." Writing, too, was a world of "Thou shall nots" instead of a world of possibility.

Performance in her school band was a positive outlet for Sarah. When Sarah was in elementary school, the band director talked to each class and invited each child to join the band. Like Julia, Sarah emphasized the importance of being "invited" into other worlds. Responding to an invitation to be included in the world of music, Sarah said, "I found something that I could do, that I felt good about." Winning awards, Sarah remained in band throughout high school because, as she observed, "the hesitancy and reluctance and fear of performing and memorization did not seem to translate *as strongly* in music because I felt successful in my own right in music. I had a confidence level, and I felt assured." She also performed in several school musicals, but "mostly in the chorus, just in behind-the-scenes, fun-type parts that did not have to be done *perfectly*."

Sarah was always told by teachers and parents that she did not work up to her "*potential*," a word that visibly angered her when she recalled its use. By being constantly told by teachers and parents that she had "potential," Sarah realized that she was "probably very intelligent," but she recognized that she was not interested in "producing the *kind* of work the institutions demanded": perfect replication of knowledge, appearance, and behavior. To Sarah, "a person who worked to his or her potential made all A's; that was the yardstick." Sarah was always in the "college-bound group," a group of students which at that time was pre-determined, according to Sarah, by the income level and social class of their parents and "what they [their parents] could do for them." As was the case with Beverly, college was "expected" for Sarah; "*it was just the next phase of life*." Sarah went to college with poor study skills, and she went from a world of "no freedom to a world of too much freedom." She explained that she would have been "doomed to fail" had she not met her future husband during her first semester because she had to make choices on her own. He helped her "know what some of the boundaries were." She completed 2 years of college, and then she got married.

During her freshman year, she took a class for students "who did not have good writing skills." She recalled, "A gentle and encouraging lady took the time to teach and not make me feel bad if I did not do well." Sarah explained that she still felt fear in this teacher's class, but because she "*liked*" the teacher, she performed better. In terms of the teacher's pedagogical approach, Sarah noted that the teacher's "mode of thinking was more forgiving" than the rule-based mode to which she had been exposed in the past. "She showed us the *structure*, but she showed us how to bend the rules. She told us to play around a bit," Sarah remembered.

That Sarah, with so much talent and "potential," was shaped in so many rote worlds and not allowed to "play around a bit" creatively made her life difficult. Her potential, it seems, never found a matching institutional home for its development. Sarah did not have a nurturing mentor during her formative years with whom to talk about her conflicting feelings—talk that might have allowed a more positive reflection of self. Sarah was the product of middle-class expectations. When she rebelled by refusing to do boring assignments or by having friends from other socioeconomic classes, she suffered. She disappointed adults, and she was excluded from her peers. Sarah shared her beliefs that women tend to form cliques that are socioeconomically based: "Women are selected for admittance because they will feed the self-perceptions of the other women in the group. Those who do not fit this perception are excluded." Even though Sarah possessed the socioeconomic capital to fit in, she felt shut out because she knew that she wanted to speak and pursue her own avenue of thinking and behaving. To do so, however, would have been to act incorrectly, and those in charge of the institutions that were shaping her expected the creation of a correct Sarah. She has spent almost 40 years fighting silently, trying not to shut down; like Beverly, only now is she finding the freedom to be herself. But modifying perceptions is difficult, and the fear of failure is strong and always present.

A tactile learner, Sarah told me that she is "very good at taking something that has to be put together and assembling it." She laughingly told me about one job that she had in a bank: "I figured out how to make that computer do things the bank officials didn't want me to know." Institutional insistence on the transmission of knowledge instead of the construction of knowledge seriously attempted to shut down Sarah's instinctive style of learning and of approaching the world. However, Sarah is struggling to find new safe places for expression and acceptance. In her current church, she has found an institution that will allow her to be herself.

Beverly and Sarah had material comforts and financial and educational advantages, but neither felt free to be herself. Both found that being in the background was a safe place to be, for inadequacies and imperfections might be not be seen there. The constant burden of trying to be correct has silenced them in some ways. Perhaps they have feared losing their perceived status or correct background or their circle of friends. But both desperately want freedom to be themselves. In the words of Sarah, they want to be "who they really are and okay with that, healthy people who don't have to pretend to be other than who they are."

The invisible yet powerful expectations of a "perfect, correct, and real" person can create a literacy paralysis—in terms of reading, writing, or speaking—in persons from all walks of life within U.S. society. Many are silenced for fear of revealing themselves in a world seeming to demand an unobtainable perfection, a reality constructed by media images, symbols, and the accouterments of a proper background. Sadly, literacy is used to fuel the creation of this constructed perception of perfection. J. Elspeth Stuckey (1991) argues that literacy does not necessarily empower all people, for it is too much a tool of middle- and upper-middle class concerns. Yet, one hope for freeing ourselves from a perception of *correct* people and the arrogance that keeps that perception alive is to use literacy for the purpose of voicing our opinions and thoughts, to engage in reflective writing, reading, and dialogue: To not shut down even when we feel shut out.

Unfortunately, using literacy to that end is not as easy as it might seem. One must be taught early that one may use literacy to empower oneself. As part of a person's background, he or she must be taught that making mistakes is part of learning and growth and that learning takes place outside schools in forms other than just rote memorization.

Angel's Story

Angel's story depicts a woman who possesses a disposition for learning beyond memorization. She has had many opportunities to shut down, but she has refused to be silenced. In her recollections of school, she recalls being the object of arrogant perception because of class. Angel, however, fought back. She knew that she could read and write, and she was not afraid to use literacy to excel. She believed in her own ability and in her right to be herself.

Angel, who is 40, was born in a southern community known for its textile mills and tobacco industry. "Everybody knew everybody," Angel told me. "I wasn't just my mom's child; I was everybody's child." Angel grew up in a world orchestrated by friendship, love, and understanding, a safe place in many ways. The larger world around her, though, was not so safe. It was the rural South in the 1960s, a world of limited opportunity for this African American female. Her father disappeared when she was young. She greatly respects her mother, who could not work due to poor health; it is from her mother that Angel believes she got her "fighting spirit, strength, and backbone."

Angel's mother was "on social services, on welfare," but Angel stated that they were not "poor-poor." In fact, Angel acknowledged that while "money wasn't coming out of everywhere," they "never wanted for anything," for they grew their own vegetables, and her mother canned food for them. Her mother struggled to provide for them and to encourage her children to get an education. Angel said, "We did not know what it was to go hungry or to be cold, for whenever my mother's children went out, we were dressed just as well as other kids." She recalled an Easter when she was about 12 years old. A girlfriend took Angel to her house to show her a new outfit laid out upon her bed. Angel feared up until Easter morning that she would not have a new dress and shoes; however, on Easter morning, a beautiful dress, high heels, and a heart-shaped birthstone necklace, all provided by her mother, were on her bed. Angel's mother *made her feel special and loved*; she readily sacrificed for her. This early lesson is a critical component in the creation of a disposition for learning and, subsequently, one's willingness to use literacy in everyday life confidently rather than just as escape routes from a life challenged by fear and intimidation.

Angel was the salutatorian at her eighth-grade graduation, and she had excellent high school grades. But Angel knew that she did not have much of a future in a southern mill town. After she married she worked in the mills for a short time to support her own children. "I went to work with a scarf on my head to keep the lint out of my hair," she said, "and I even covered my feet with plastic bread bags to walk to work in the snow, because I could not afford to buy shoes for my children and for myself." Angel did not want to be a "welfare mom," and she realized that if she stayed in her hometown, there would be no "better jobs."

Therefore, her major challenge in life was to move from this small town, where she was surrounded by friends and family and love, to the large, cosmopolitan city where she now resides. She recalled that in her hometown, "there were more people trying to help you than trying to pull you back. Those who tried to pull you back were more or less the people my own age who weren't trying to do for themselves. They were scared if you made it, they would look bad." According to Angel, who became a single parent when she and her husband divorced, "This move offered me a chance to provide for myself and my family economically. I believed that I should be able to go for myself and not look for handouts. It is a better feeling to know what you've accomplished, what you've worked for."

Angel attended college and worked with computers until she experienced a life-threatening illness. Working had enabled her to be "financially set with benefits and insurance." When she became ill, coworkers donated their own sick leave to help Angel until she became financially stable. One coworker, a college graduate and supervisor, explained to Angel their reasons for helping her, "You deserve it because you're a good person. And I know that if the shoe were on the other foot, you'd do it for me."

In her community, Angel is respected because of her positive attitude and perseverance. She told me that she is "grateful to be alive" and that she is basically happy. She sees her health problems as "small" compared to those of others. Being a "people person," she does admit to being "lonesome," now that she is not working and going out into the world every day.

Although she recalls moving to the city as her major challenge in life, the move was a trade-off in many ways. Angel compared city life to country life. She noted that in the neighborhood where she resides now, there is "no brotherly love." She described a defensive, alienated community. Children are not corrected by other adults in the community; if they are, their parents get angry and defend their children's actions, whether the actions are appropriate or not. There are no common codes for behavior shared by families; each family lives in isolation in its own apartment. She recalled her own mother's friends "*visiting* over coffee, *talking* and *trusting* each other with confidences, and going downtown to shop or buy groceries and *sharing* cab fares." Although she finds neither trustworthiness nor reciprocity in her culturally diverse neighborhood, she did recall these traits in those with whom she worked in the city.

During our interviews, Angel frequently quoted her mother. For example, "If a task is once begun, be it great or small, do it right or not at all." Angel, the fighter, seemed to internalize her mother's values and sense of ethics. She admitted that she is always quoting something, because when she was growing up, those were the words repeated by the adults to the children. Her mother frequently told Angel and her siblings about the "things that had happened in the family, family stories about Grandmother or Great-grandmother." Her immediate family and her extended family still talk to each other: They phone, they write letters, and once a year the extended family gets together in the hometown for a family reunion. At this event, according to Angel, "The older members talk about how it was in the old days. And then we, the next generation, talk about how we remember it. And then my children hear it; they hear the stories of their family." Oral history is a critical aspect of Angel's life; family stories and values are passed in this manner from generation to generation.

When Angel grew up, her family did not have a television set. Therefore, for entertainment, they not only told stories, they read. Angel read everything that she could get her hands on: comic books, westerns, classics, and a catechism. While reading aloud to the oldest child, her mother also taught and inspired the other children who sat at her feet listening. Watching her older brother read made Angel want to read. Her mother taught her children "to spell words out— to sound them out—and then spell them and read them." Angel now teaches her young godchild to read in the same manner. "Also, when she's reading to me," Angel said, "I define words as we go because it's bad for a person to use a word and not know what it means." Angel's mother also "*expected*" all A's and B's; she went over her children's homework with them. While doing their homework, the children read to their mother. Angel teaches as her mother taught.

The interrelatedness of home, church, and school in Angel's childhood community allowed literacy acts in one institution to be constantly transferred and transmuted to other contexts. Angel recalled playing school and church; however, her memories of playing church are more vivid, and she is quite honest in her recollections that the children "imitated and even made fun of" the adults' church rituals through their play. Angel and the other children watched the prayer bands, groups of older church women, as they met at homes on a weekly basis because in the 1950s they did not yet have a church building. At these meetings, the women washed one another's feet, sang, testified, and then prayed. In their testimonies, they "talked about how good God had been." The scenes and sounds are recorded in Angel's mind: "While they washed each other's feet, they were quiet. Then they would start talking and testifying and singing and praying and shouting. At that point, they got their tambourines and began shouting and jumping."

When the children played, Angel never assumed the role of the preacher, for men were preachers; rather, she assumed a female role of shouter. She recalled, "We remembered *how* they prayed, and if they got stuck on something and kept repeating it over and over and over again, we thought that was funny. So we would imitate the praying: 'Father, Father, Father...We want to thank you, thank you, thank you ....' We would really get into that part of it, and then we'd start shouting and jumping." During play, Angel internalized the oral literacy practices of the church, an important institution in the life of her family and community. Like Ella, Angel only played roles that she saw women assume.

Angel recalled that her church first met in tents, with the prayer bands meeting regularly in homes. Funds were procured for a basement, and eventually a church structure was completed. The congregation read Sunday school books at church, but Angel recalled recitation and performance as the most salient literacy events. Children in Angel's church were encouraged to learn Bible verses and recite them. During a competition, of sorts, members of the church selected a representative to go to different churches and compete. First, second, and third prizes were awarded, and Angel remembered winning for her church by reciting 5 Matthew. She said that she seemed to know that she was going to win because she always "recited, recited, recited."

Memorization, recitation, and reading were also important aspects of Angel's elementary schooling. She attended a typical elementary school, which at that time and place had no kindergarten. She reiterated, "Everybody knew everybody. The teachers knew your mama; in fact, the teachers probably taught your mama!" The perceptions of these teachers "who knew everybody and their mothers" influenced her grades and her attitude about school. Her competitive spirit and her astute observations of school politics and teacher arrogance, however, propelled her to persevere and not shut down. She became determined to prove to her teachers that she could excel in her schoolwork. Angel concluded our interview about school literacy stating, "I remember all the teachers I had in elementary school—some of them were very nice and some of them were very mean—but *they shaped us, the kids of my time.*" Indeed, each teacher seemed to have contributed to shaping Angel's perceptions of herself.

She began by discussing first-grade reading. "We used to pair up and read," she said "because we didn't have enough books or maybe they thought that two heads were better than one. I had learned to read at home, but at school we read *Stop Run Jane Run See Dick Run Stop Stop Stop*—all that stuff. By third grade, we didn't pair up any more, and by third grade I had to sit right in front of the teacher—because I talked all the time."

Angel's first-grade teacher was "mean," and according to Angel, "All the teachers were friends, so one opinion of a student got passed on to the next." In fact, she stated, "You had a reputation before the next teacher got to you. I did talk a lot because they just didn't make it interesting for me. As punishment for talking, I used to have to spend some time in the corner [standing] on one foot with my face to the wall." I asked Angel what this did to her self-esteem and how she responded. She said, "It just *really* brought out my nasty attitude." Angel fought back in her own way; she was not particularly intimidated by the assumed power of her teachers, and she resisted silence or retreat as a response to punishment. Whereas the often bored Sarah retreated quietly into the safe fictional world of books when punished, Angel fought back with displeasing school behaviors, such as talking.

When I asked Angel more about her "reputation," obviously acquired by the end of first grade, she explained her perception of class distinctions in her school: "Since everybody knew everybody in the neighborhood, and everybody's kids came to these same elementary teachers year after year, your grades and your reputation, I guess the reputation the teachers *perceived* you to have, got passed along with your report card." Angel continued, "My mom always made sure we did our homework. We always had our lessons. But I was one of those the teachers did not particularly like, I guess, because my mom was on social services and, being on social services, people had this idea *that people on welfare were supposed to be a certain way. And we were not the way they thought that people on welfare should be. And because of that, I think, the teachers resented that we did well in school. They believed that since we were on welfare, we were not supposed to be able to learn; we were supposed to come to school looking like we were on welfare.*"

According to Angel, the first-grade teacher solidified her reputation with most of the other teachers—with the critical exception of her third-grade teacher. Her elementary school was racially segregated, and she added, "It was a social class thing. There's not just prejudice *between* races; there's prejudice *in* races, too. And I think that's the worst kind." With the help of her kind third-grade teacher, Angel refused to be silenced or shut out of school, a world controlled by members of another social class. As a small child, Angel believed that middle-class teachers really believed those on welfare could not learn. Unfortunately, Ella, when describing her encounter with her child's teachers, has the same powerful perception of some middle-class teachers.

Angel's third-grade teacher, however, "loved" her and, like Angel's mother, encouraged her and had high expectations for her. Angel recalled, *"This woman graded me on my work, not on my family."* Angel described her: "She was kind and loving. She wasn't the kind of person who went into the classroom and talked about students—you know how some teachers have a way of talking to their students and making them feel down or not good enough. They are stuffy; they turn up their noses—those types of people." Angel's defense against an arrogant, "stuffy" person was to "do whatever it takes to aggravate that person."

Angel did not have to "aggravate" the third-grade teacher, and that year Angel made the honor roll beginning a consistent pattern. That 1 year of academic achievement also seemed to be fueled by what Angel described as "competition," a belief that, "Hey, I can do it, too." Incredibly astute, she observed that her teachers' children and the teachers' "pets" got "special treatment and often better grades—passed along." Angel never gave up, though, and became the salutatorian of her elementary school. Her responses to types of attempted shutdown seem to be shaped by context. In relationships, when she senses being used or being treated unfairly, she will speak out about the perceived injustice.

Angel loved elementary school poetry recitations and plays, because she excelled in recitation at school, as she did at church. Once a month on a Friday evening, the teachers and students held a program at the school, a literacy event. Everyone's parents came, dressed in Sunday clothes; Angel compared it "to going out to a theater."

Angel still loves poetry and, during our interview, she recited some of the poems she learned 30 years ago; her eyes lit up during this part of the interview. She knew the odds of being picked to recite for the Friday night performances, but she also knew that she could do it. Every month, each student recited the same poem, and the teachers would select the "best" performer. After years of watching the pattern of this ritual, Angel surmised that the teachers often "went out of their way to pick their own children or their peers' children." Angel decided to compete and simply prove that she was the best. She recited some of "January's poem," which she believed to be titled "Somebody's Mother": "The woman was old and raggedy and gray/ And bent with the chill of a cold winter's day." Then she recalled all of "February's poem," which she believed to be titled "Race Pride."

Angel did not recall stigmatization or racial prejudice during her high school years and, unlike Ella, Angel found opportunity waiting in a larger school not in her community. She continued to excel, and she always loved English. She "just loved diagramming—breaking those sentences down." She also loved reading so much that she used to read books for other students, write their book reports, and charge them for the service. Other than book reports, Angel did not recall much about writing in high school; however, she did recall writing in her college courses. Having been out of high school several years before attending college, Angel used the same fighting spirit to pass her courses and excel. She noted that all of her college teachers "*believed*" that she could do the work; one male teacher, who encouraged her, told her to get her priorities straight and get an education. After he explained that the choice for passing was up to the students, Angel remembered, "I would go to sleep with my textbook, and I would wake up with it on my face, and I can remember taking it with me to work and, on my lunch hour, I would have a cup of coffee and a pack of crackers because I was studying." Enabled by a strong, internalized ethic, strong reading skills, and a belief that she was capable of doing the work, she did not quit. She again had found a teacher who graded on her work, not her background. Her success in her college courses later affected her success on her job positively.

Angel frequently writes letters, and she is still an avid reader. One day we talked about her favorite books, which were *Makes Me Wanna Holler*, *Waiting to Exhale*, and *A Lesson Before Dying*. She discussed Terry McMillan's *Waiting to Exhale* at length. Describing it as a book about everyday life, she continued, "It's everyday life and the changes that women go through trying to form a relationship and falling for the wrong man and just trying to find somebody that's going to treat them right and be there for them. And she [McMillan] just *put it in a book and let you know that when you're going through it, you can know that you're not the only one*."

A gift from her brother, Nathan McCall's *Makes Me Wanna Holler* is probably her favorite book. She explained, "As a single parent raising black males, I didn't have that perspective, a male perspective. I needed that. I raised my sons the way I thought they should be, but this book made me see a lot of things that my sons tried to tell me that I couldn't understand. I think if my sons would read it, it would help them understand a lot of the things that I tried to tell them from my point of view. It would help them understand. They used to say to me, 'Nag, nag, nag...all the time.' But I think if they took the time to read the book, they would understand why I feel the way I do." One son has begun reading it at the encouragement of his uncle and his mother. Angel's connection to these books is actually summarized by McCall's (1994) own "encounter with Richard Wright." McCall explained, "It blew my mind to think that somebody could take words that described exactly how I felt and put them together in a story like that" (p. 165); McCall stated in his book that he had his "reality validated" by reading Wright's work, as has Angel in McCall's and McMillan's writing. In fact, Angel has not only had her "reality validated" in words, she has also found the reflective mirror of the reality of others—males, for example—allowing her to understand multiple viewpoints and their validity.

Currently, Angel is concerned with the oral and pictorial messages that children are receiving from their peers, their music, and television. She believes that the images children are receiving from electronic media—images and messages of "violence, guns, and female bashing"—conflict with the deeply instilled messages that she, as did her mother and teachers, is still teaching orally. Angel stated, "Their heads are being filled with [these messages]; they are hearing them. And the people who are filling their heads [with them] are doing it in a way that the kids can relate to because they are doing it in rap." Angel seems to be at war with new literacy technology, which dramatically competes for the attention of children. She believes that children are drawn to messages that conflict with the values she is trying to teach. When asked what advice she'd give to English teachers, Angel responded, "Plays, performance, songs! If it's something they enjoy, you'll see them rapping, beating, bopping, talking because they've got it. They've got it!" She thinks that teachers should use this new technology and compete for the attention of children.

When Angel performed, she "got it," retained it, and internalized it, as evidenced by her performance for me without practice in 30 years. She also loved to read and learned that reading was entertainment when she read with her family for the pure delight of it. School reading, at least in the first few grades, was decontextualized "stuff" that neither connected with life-at-large nor "validated any life experiences," and it bored the very bright Angel to the extent that she became a "problem" (or perhaps "more of a problem" than she would have been already because of the complexity of the factors in her early school life). Angel believed that her first-grade teacher did not like her because of her social class. However, another problem was that the teachers in Angel's school were probably using the only materials they had; perhaps as Ella described, the books used and their scarcity were due to racial educational inequalities during the 1950s and 1960s. Although Angel did not shut down and did not perceive herself as "too old to fix," she is aware of the danger of boring students, of not connecting with their life experiences. In essence, she alerts us that teachers may shut out people because they are not merging knowledge, stories, and positive messages with the technology available, technology

73

that might help children "get it." Schools relying on antiquated texts instead of computers and electronic media for example, may be guilty of creating more children, who when they are confronted with the reality of the disparity in their educational backgrounds, may cry out, "We are doomed."

Angel is obviously quite resilient. She also was reared by a mother who persevered and who valued reading and education. She was disciplined at home, but she had creative outlets and was free to play and to challenge the status quo. She felt loved and valued at an early age. Although Angel obviously spent much precious school time in the corner, facing the wall and standing on one foot, she chose neither to "passively shut down" (Fine, 1992) nor to slide safely into the background under a defensive guise termed "average" by Rose (1990). With the help of a teacher who was not arrogant, she experienced academic and personal success for a year—one critical year that redirected her energy and fueled future academic success.

Edna's Story

When I first sat down with 70-year-old Edna at her kitchen table and heard her talk, I soon realized that any story she recounted was naturally bound in some way to the acts of reading and writing. Edna perceived that literacy—reading and writing and what these acts made possible— had been important keys to her personal growth; she attributed her self-confidence specifically to reading. Edna chose her pseudonym quickly because of her love of Edna St. Vincent Millay's poetry (and like Angel, with no prompting, she immediately recalled and quoted some for me). Although Edna never completed her dream of graduating from college and teaching, she revealed that she has taught others to read and write during her journey through life, and what she teaches is her passion for mastering knowledge, and for using literacy to empower and better oneself. Like Angel, Edna has resisted shutting down even when she has been shut out. She recalled a few instances of being perceived arrogantly, but because of her self-confidence and her belief in her own self-worth, she just chose to move on.

A white woman from the South, Edna described her place of birth: "It was a gracious, charming southern city. We had a mixture of people there; some of the most intelligent women educators were born there. The city at that time was very cosmopolitan for a southern city. It had small-town ideas—everybody knew everybody—but it had cosmopolitan ideas, too. I remember hearing Rachmaninoff as a girl. I came to know later that I had been exposed to a very outstanding background knowledge because of the community."

Edna's parents divorced when she was a toddler, and her mother remarried several years later. Around 1927, her family moved to a predominantly Catholic neighborhood and lived upstairs in a house they shared with another family. Edna recalled most of the families in this new neighborhood as "wonderful people, lace curtain Irish, very well educated, and delightful to know." Edna was reared by not only her mother, but also her aunt, her aunt's flamboyant friend and her "self-made" husband, and two African American women who worked for the family, and yet were "family." Edna valued these women and their strength; she believes that they all "shaped" the person she has become.

Today, Edna believes that her family of origin would be described as "dysfunctional"; however, her family was extremely close and loving although, in Edna's mind, it was atypical for the time and place. Her many female mentors were all deeply religious women, but her mother, her aunt, and their friend were not "church-going" people because she said, "Protestants would not have accepted them." The three women thus were ostracized in some ways in the white community. But they sent Edna to church alone each Sunday, and she doggedly went and found a place she would always love. In many ways, these women lived out their dreams of success and upward mobility through their expectations for Edna. The flamboyant friend made plans during Edna's high school years to send her to a private boarding school in another country; however, Edna's mother refused to allow Edna to be taken so far from her even for this cultural exposure. This same friend helped Edna's mother dress Edna in expensive clothes, shoes, and hats; Edna shared that it was "ingrained" in her from an early age that one should wear fine clothes, for one's taste "would set you off as knowing quality things."

Edna shared an extensive family history with me, most of which had been preserved by the storytelling art of her aunt and by family photos (which she also shared with me). Her grandfather's family "lost everything in the War between the States." Therefore, she explained, "Moneywise, I grew up very poor during the Depression in the South, but we were rich in values and love." Her mother and father had no formal education, but Edna repeatedly described her mother as a highly intelligent woman, who worked hard her entire life and "who was ahead of her time." When her parents divorced, her enterprising mother got a job in a fine department store and "made more money than the average man at that time."

Edna stated that she has never felt "inferior," and she attributed her self-confidence to two factors: her extensive reading over the years and her loving and accepting family. She said she realizes now that during the Depression years her mother and aunt frequently fed her and the children first because there was not enough food for the entire family. The Depression and an illness resulted in Edna being unable to attend college after high school, and she got a job with her mother in the department store earning $10 per week, five of which went to help her mother. Edna always "observed" others whom she described as "well bred and well educated." Frequently, she recalled that she and her mother were dinner guests of store officials; she commented, "That's how I learned to be at ease in fine restaurants and meetings. I observed and did exactly as they did; I noticed how they acted. On the other hand, my mother made sure we never associated with vulgar people—coarse, vulgar people who didn't read and who didn't go to church." As Brandt (1995) found in her literacy research, to Edna's mother, "the ability to read was...an indication of moral behavior itself" (p. 654).

Edna married during World War II and left the South. Her husband decided to make the military a career after he was recalled for the Korean War, and a military life enabled Edna to travel extensively. She attributed her success in being able to "mingle from the highest to the lowest" to extensive reading and experience working in a department store, where she, like her mother, learned to "read" people. Her mother, she noted, frequently told her children that "Working in a department store was her college education, a place where she learned about psychology, people, and life." Edna also commented on her southern accent: "When you're with another southerner, you may use it, but you find with a diversified group, you don't. And then you gradually lose it." Edna recalled that the people in the North with whom she worked commented on her "pronunciation," but she accepted their chiding good-naturedly. She then quickly "lost it."

During her husband's career, Edna noted unapologetically, "I was the rock who made a home so that my husband could leave for years at a time and not worry." Learning to adapt to new places and new situations, she also handled all the finances and, when her husband died suddenly at an early age, she added, "I became strong and more centered on myself." She returned to college after his death and eventually accrued 60 hours of college credits; however, life events always stopped her from completing the degree. For a brief period, Edna lived with her daughter while her daughter attended college and, during this time, Edna often "sneaked" in to lecture classes, knowing that "one more student wouldn't make any difference." Although Edna has a respect for "correctness," she has displayed a daring, an ability to take risks probably learned from the women who reared her and showed her how to survive. Unlike Sarah, Edna learned as a child that structure was important, but she grew up observing loving women around her "bending the rules." During this unofficial college stint, she especially loved her courses in children's literature and linguistics. Of that time period, Edna said, "We had a great time. After the lectures, I'd go to the library and read and look around. *Never a dull moment.*" The enterprising Edna was not shut out from formal education; she invited herself.

Edna never recalled any recollections of shutting down in her life; she had been taught to keep going by the indefatigable women who surrounded her. Laughing, she did recall being shut out of one church. In the 1950s she and her husband had been assigned to live near a prestigious New England college. Edna explained, "I didn't really know too much about the liberals' view of military people—what I would call the 'Harvard view.' We just looked up the nearest Presbyterian church to attend, and it was in an exclusive neighborhood. My husband wore his uniform to church, and we were more or less told that we were not wanted there. The minister, who had graduated from Yale, was adamant; his sermon was directed at us. We never went back." Edna chuckled over the incident, but she did not let this experience keep her from church.

Edna's "dysfunctional" but loving family, her extensive reading, her observations of survival during the Depression, and the frequent requirement to move and assimilate during military life with her husband contributed to shaping a woman who believes that she has "mingled from the highest to the lowest and *been accepted*." She said that reading gave her things to talk about and allowed her to envision other worlds. Growing up in the South during the Depression, she remembered poor farmers, people living in cabins, and yet she stated, "I've been accepted by them. You can tell, you know, if you are. They are very proud, too. And then in the highest society, I remember attending a reception for the Japanese Emperor!" Edna currently lives with her daughter and her family. Her major role in life is to make sure her grandchildren get a "*good moral background and a good education*." The two are correlated in Edna's mind, and Edna is concerned about the world in which her grandchildren are growing up: It is a world in which people are "too hurried" for manners and, according to Edna, "*Manners are part of one's background*."

After discussing the word "background" so extensively with Beverly, I also asked Edna to talk about the term because it appeared repeatedly on her transcripts, and she often made references to class distinctions. In her definition she connected her perception of background and class to one's manners. She stated, "*Manners are how to make people that you are with feel comfortable regardless of your station. You don't look up; you don't look down. You make them feel comfortable*." Edna seemed to accept the reality that people do look "up and down" and that one does seem to have a "station" in life, but she emphasized the importance of not being arrogant in the presence of one who, in Julia's words, has "less-than" others.

When Edna recalled her childhood, she discussed her father: "You would have thought he was English aristocracy, very well educated. He wrote a beautiful letter with beautiful handwriting. He was well versed on anything anyone brought up to discuss—a very *cosmopolitan* type of man. We used to say, 'How did a poor boy from the mountains get these ideas?' But they just seemed natural to him." The stories of this man and the observations of him focus on Brandt's (1995) description of a "literacy of gentility and upward mobility" allowing one to associate "language correctness and good breeding," an ideology still prevalent in the South and an ideology that has permeated Edna's sense of literacy and its purposes in her life—and in her grandchildren's lives.

Edna's sense of literacy and its power was influenced greatly by one of the wealthier Irish families in the Catholic neighborhood where she grew up. The patriarch of this family owned an island, and every summer he would gather all the neighborhood children, load them into his covered vehicle, and regularly transport them there for outings. During the trips, Edna recalled, he recited "lengthy epic poems that he had recited as a boy" including Longfellow's *The Wreck of the Hesperus*. Around 1930, this same man owned the first radio in the neighborhood, and "he invited *all the children*"—regardless of "their station"—to hear a broadcast that Edna recalled came from Cincinnati, Ohio. Every child was allowed to wear earphones and listen for several minutes. He kept asking the children, "Can you hear it? Can you hear it?" Edna added, "That was the most thrilling thing!" During the summer, he and his family would sit on their front porch and read Shakespeare, and when people visited, their 5-year-old grandson recited Shakespeare for the guests on the porch. In his large home, Edna remembered an enormous upstairs hallway lined with bookshelves from "floor to ceiling." These shelves held "classics," which Edna did not have at home; however, she said, "I was allowed regularly to borrow any books that I wanted to read, and then I returned them and got more." One of the daughters in this same family began her career as a teacher in the town and eventually became a school principal. In the summers she was "in charge of the neighborhood playground." She taught softball and basketball and directed plays. Every day she had a story hour, and the children would gather to hear her read "wonderful stories." Edna noted, *"You could hear her booming voice all over. She was dynamic."*

Another strong female voice in her memory, this woman demonstrated to Edna that women were teachers of literacy, fully expected to learn classical literature, and that women participated in sports, plays, and life. She taught Edna that white women could be participants in mainstream U.S. culture. Her wealthy and well-educated family encouraged the intellectual growth of the white children in the neighborhood regardless of their financial situation or class. Edna was quite honest in her recollections of racial prejudice and segregated schools, stores, and neighborhoods; the opportunities for upward mobility were quite different for African Americans and whites in this time and place.

Although many of Edna's early literacy experiences were orchestrated by the wealthy and well-educated neighbors whom she so much admired, Edna's home was filled with racially, socioeconomically, and religiously diverse people who engaged in literacy use and Nancie Atwell's (1987) now well-known "literacy talk." Edna's reality was actually made up of "multiple realities." When they were young, she and her brother stayed at home with her aunt and the two deeply religious African American women. These three women were storytellers and, according to Edna, cooked and ironed in the kitchen and talked away the hours. Edna heard tales of her father's rise from poverty to cultural accomplishment and then to abandonment of her family. She heard the African American women tell tales of their own "skunks of misery," men who had abandoned them. In her own home, she recalled that daily everyone read two newspapers "cover to cover," and every issue was debated when her uncle joined them in the evenings for dinner. The children were encouraged to voice their opinions. Edna recalled, "The books in our house were light reading, such as books by Zane Grey and Kathleen Norris and, of course, we had a set of encyclopedias." Her literacy experiences were enhanced later by the introduction of silent movies and radio; she proudly recalled reading aloud to her aunt the lines of script on the movie screen.

Like Angel and Sarah, Edna knew how to read before she started to school, but she skipped the first half of first grade. Her older brother, who played school with her, always assumed the role of teacher and, by the time Edna started to school, she knew the entire first-grade curriculum. She laughingly recalled being labeled "not conservative" by her mother because of the "realistic" books by Ayn Rand her mother learned that Edna was reading as a teenager. The books did not contain profanity; however, they were written "so differently from the books that her mother's generation had read" that they caused her mother to be alarmed. Edna read them in spite of her mother's disapproval and discussed Rand's ideas with the family.

When questioned about writing at home, Edna, like most of the other research participants, faltered momentarily. She asked, "What do you mean by writing? Essays?" After some discussion, she recalled, "I wrote poems as a young girl and, of course, we always did our homework." She added that she did not recall anyone "writing per se except for letters—lots of letters."

Writing and reading and discussion (critical exploration, connection to current political events, connection to family history and experiences) now are part of everyday life at Edna's home, where she lives with her daughter and grandchildren. These aspects of life are highly interrelated and often spring from the still-respected and valued homework assignments that the grandchildren receive at their private school. Edna serves as the homework facilitator because both parents are employed. Edna also previously volunteered in the writing program at the grandchildren's public school. As the anecdote that follows illustrates, her experience there revealed an ideological-moral conflict manifesting itself in school literacy and the methods being used to teach reading and writing. Following this experience, her grandchildren were moved to a traditional private school.

When Edna's older grandchild was in public elementary school, Edna and her daughter visited the school periodically to read student writing samples. Edna described the experience: "We were reading the portfolio contents, which were things—things because they could not be categorized as very much of anything. They had no punctuation, no semblance of form. The students had been allowed to write anything they wanted to." She added, "One [piece] that I tried to look over was 'How to Murder Your Teacher.'" This piece of writing was directed to the 10-year-old writer's teacher. Shocked, Edna asked the teacher for advice on how to comment on the writing and how to "correct" it. According to Edna, the teacher said, *Just lead the students into a method of making sense of their writing.*

This method of dealing with student writing in no way corresponded to the way that Edna or her daughter had been taught. Edna had frequently assisted her own children in their writing assignments, and they had always gotten excellent "marks" on their essays on topics such as Russian literature. They had never contemplated on paper how to murder their teachers. Edna explained that she had been taught "forms" for paragraphs and themes and essays: a beginning, a body, a conclusion, and a title. Edna recalled two specific situations in which she assisted her children with major school papers in which Edna had stressed aspects of organization, form, and the need for "catchy titles." The content, of course, was morally appropriate.

Unhappy with Edna's grandson's "background in writing," his parents moved him to a private school "where writing was considered important." Edna described the child's first year in contrast to his previous elementary school years: *He had to write essay after essay, book report after book report. And he was lost.* Edna, the facilitator of homework in the household, said, "I did not want to teach him in the wrong way." "I studied right along with him, and we learned together from his book." Her disposition for learning, for tackling the content of a new book was evident, and she modeled this attitude for her grandson.

Before studying her grandson's English book with him, Edna analyzed her own writing skills and how she had been taught to write. Although she realized that she had been taught "form," she asked herself if her own writing was not "just off the top of her head." She questioned the "correctness" of her own writing, because in studying his textbook, she realized that a "step-by-step method was outlined," one which she assumed was the "correct way," because it was a text sanctioned by an educational institution that the family respected. Observing that her grandson had "great ideas," she also analyzed his learning style, for his ideas were frequently "shortened" in order for him to get his thoughts on paper and be on his way to other tasks. "A scientific type," he disliked assignments with length requirements. Edna took him to the library and helped him select reference books on his topics. Together they perused the books, finding ideas; Edna taught him to outline this reading and to take notes. *"Then,"* Edna stated, *"we would start writing."* Edna used this method herself. I observed her at a meeting when she shared her notes and an extensive outline that had been cross-referenced by page numbers with the text and additional sources from which she had supplemented the lesson being studied. When members of the group commented about her dedication to the lesson, Edna laughingly responded, "I'm teaching my grandson to do this and, therefore, I'm doing it, too." Edna, assuming the role of teacher, naturally tried to analyze her grandson's metacognitive approach to writing, and then she modeled a learning process that she wanted him to emulate.

With Edna's help, her grandson won several essay contests and has excelled in the new school, but only after "catching up"—after quickly learning the *"background,"* which all the other children in the private school possessed—a *background* believed to be necessary for upward mobility, moral development, and educational success. In this new school environment, Edna has helped him with his reading, also. She recalled his reading of Charles Dickens; after the first 15 pages, he told Edna he "hated all those words" and the length of the book. He also told Edna that Dickens could say what was needed in order to communicate without wasting so many words. At this point, Edna began to read short sections from Dickens aloud to him on a daily basis and then discuss what they had read by comparing the poverty of the era with the Great Depression that she had experienced. She said that he did not fully understand the historical period and culture of Dickens's works, but that he really enjoyed their time together and their talks. Her son-in-law criticized her reading aloud to her grandson; he stated emphatically that his son "should be reading for himself!" However, Edna and her daughter decided that because he "was listening and getting it," Edna could continue to read to him. Her granddaughter soon demanded equal and private reading time with Edna.

On the refrigerator in the kitchen, I noted magnets holding messages and notes. Edna's magnets held a "Books I Have Read" list and a book report instruction form. Always a learner and a teacher, Edna explained, "The children and I work together because I love to read everything, and I enjoy almost everything they bring home. They had a Great Books program when they were in public school, but...the program was very haphazard. They read maybe one book that whole year in their so-called Great Books Program. In their private school, though, the librarian meets with the children every week and assigns them so many pages per week to read. They have to ask three questions and look up words from their vocabulary list."

Edna's home is filled with talk about books, which is critical to fostering a love of books and an "understanding of literacy" (Dahl & Freppon, 1995); Edna seems to be a literacy catalyst for the family. She encourages wide reading from a variety of sources, a discussion of multiple viewpoints, and a connection of textual material to real life experiences. However, the school literacy deemed superior allows for only certain types of expression and for the transmission of a knowledge base, which forms an appropriate "background" for academic success, moral development, and upward mobility. The appropriate literacy mirrors that of Edna's Catholic neighbors whom she so admired.

Reading was always so much a part of Edna's life that she had trouble isolating reading memories pertaining to school. She could not recall a time when she did not know how to read, and she stated, "I don't remember very much about reading in the elementary grades at all; it was so natural, and I had already read most of the books." For the child who "just automatically knew how to read and to write," Edna's first memories of writing at school were of "spending so many hours with the Spencerian way of teaching handwriting," an emphasis on lovely penmanship. She did remember that teachers frequently called on her to read aloud—especially her fifth-grade teacher who encouraged Edna to become a teacher when she grew up. Edna had no fear of reading aloud.

During the Depression era, Edna recalled few private schools in her city, one girls' school and the gender-segregated Catholic schools, but she remarked that "even the well-to-do families could not afford them." Edna attended a racially segregated public school attended by children from "very humble homes" and by children who were members of "the first families in the state." Although they were racially segregated, Edna perceived her schools as socioeconomically and culturally diverse. She never recalled any favoritism by teachers of particular students. However, upon returning to this city years later, Edna noted that an established teacher in town remarked to Edna that she had taught only "the cream of the crop of [the town's] children." "This remark," Edna said, "made me start thinking—so even the teachers felt this way about the town's newer and more affluent suburbs, far from the old, downtown area in which I grew up." As a result of this conversation and hearing the "class judgment" of a teacher, Edna realized that obviously "one's whole future almost depended on the school one attended."

Edna's most salient school memory focused on a high school English teacher, who also attended her church. This teacher, known as the "professor," was also known as "the terror" and was no more pleasant at church than at school. Edna recalled, "Every child that entered high school dreaded English composition, for this teacher never gave A's." However, Edna received an A in English composition, admitting that "I don't know that I even thought about the form of things; I just wrote. I guess I had been taught form before, and it was just automatic to make it *correct*." Unlike Ella, Julia, and Sarah, Edna just wrote in school and was not afraid of being "incorrect," although her language reveals that writing was expected to be "correct." Always inquisitive and never intimidated, Edna stated that after graduation she visited the English teacher in an effort to "understand him a little better." He shared with Edna his fear that most of his students would be lost in college because of deadlines that professors expected students to meet with no prompting or reminders. Edna laughed and recalled that he said, *"My methods might seem harsh, but through my rigid training I have saved many lives in college."* Through English composition, this dreaded teacher transmitted his perceptions and expectations of self-reliance, promptness, responsibility, and correctness.

But Edna, who made an A, almost missed a deadline. The English professor had assigned a short story—with the "correct form and a given number of words"—to be turned in on a specific date. The night before it was due, a friend was talking to Edna and asked her how many words she had in her short story, which was the main grade for the course. Edna, who had forgotten the assignment, left her friend, ran home, and "dashed off" a short story. Edna explained, "I had no idea whether it was the correct *form* or not; I had no way to check it, for I did not have a book at home telling me. As part of our assignment, we were supposed to go to the library and study the correct form of the short story. But I turned it in—and I made an A. The only thing he changed was the title. And they even read it at a program for the graduating class. I was elated." She took a risk—correct form or not.

Edna took her lessons to heart. While taking college courses, she remembered helping a "young fellow" who tape recorded all the Western civilization lectures. The "poor fellow" approached Edna one day as the semester was nearing its end and asked if they could study together. Edna agreed, for the young man had to pass the exam to stay in college. Edna recalled telling him, "Well, you are going to pass this course, but put the tapes away. You've got so much information we'll be here for hours, and we don't have time because the test is in a few days." Edna continued, "So I brought my notes, and I made him *memorize* everything that I thought the teacher was going to ask on that exam—because at my age, I could study people a little bit better, and

I almost knew what the teacher was going to ask on that exam because his Ph.D. was in Russian history. So I said, 'We might have one question on World War II, but otherwise, *study Russia!*' He passed, and I got the nicest note from his mother." By studying the professor and what he knew, Edna was reading people and the institution, in addition to reading her notes. She recalled this experience as one of her greatest accomplishments: helping this young man graduate. Edna just laughs and says that she reads the world. She has learned to navigate in and through institutions to reach her goals in life.

Edna notes that although her grandchildren "do all their papers on computers and look things up on them," she is "the most computer illiterate person in the world, one who just does not get along with computers." Her grandchildren gave her a disk of her own; however, she has made a literacy decision which she explained: "I just don't like the thought of sitting and looking at a machine for hours at a time and not talking to anybody except on the computer. I like rapport with people. I can *read* people. But I don't really *read* them, I just *love* them. *I like to know what people think and feel. And you don't get that feeling on a computer.*" She has thus far resisted technology, but I noted that her grandchildren were confident that Edna could master the marvel if she so desired, and I'm sure she could. But maybe Edna has found the key to teaching people to be successful in endeavors to which literacy is integral: Just love them. Know what they think and feel.

CHAPTER 4

Shutting Out People and Resisting Shutdown: What I Heard the Women Say

This chapter is intended to reflect on the words of the women in this study and to look at the implications of their stories. As I discussed in Chapter 2, although I did as much as possible to ensure that the quotations here genuinely reflect these women's stories, I am aware that any analysis or retelling will be seen through the lens of my perceptions. I do hope, however, as Peter McLaren (1993) stated, that I have allowed the research participants to "name experience and place labels on their sense of reality" (p. 333) when describing ways in which they shut down and when explaining their reasons for doing so. By listening to how these women named experiences, I was able to sense the ways in which literacy and language are used in their everyday life. In my classes and my conferences, I find myself using their expressions when discussing a writing or reading problem with my students. The knowledge I have gained from my academic pursuits has informed me; however, the experiential knowledge of these women has made me wiser. My vocabulary has increased. In discussing the interrelation of silence, distancing, and nonreciprocity as ways of shutting down, I will use the vocabulary of the women in this study.

Although my study was limited to six women from the southern United States, by examining their narratives in depth I hoped to find out how pervasive shutdown was in their lives and what the implications of this shutdown were for literacy and language use in their life choices.

Over the course of the study, I discovered how those who are not marginalized by race or class feel about the backgrounds of those who are in some way different from them. It is not enough, in the words of Spellmeyer (1996), to discover "how people actually *feel*." Those of us in positions of power must address how we feel about those with whom we work, or our research will be no more than a contribution to what Julia saw as "*terminology and piles of paper*," which perpetuates the distance between people—students and teachers, for example. I gained insight not only into the ways people resist shutting down but also into the factors that might be explored in further research that would enable all students to be confident in their use of language and literacy.

When a person shuts down, his or her risk of nonacceptance or failure or definition by those in power by virtue of race, education, or class is reduced. Shutting down is a method by which emotional pain is avoided. It is a response that can be so subtle that it can go unnoticed by teachers. The response often is explained by teachers as a lack of motivation or "not working to one's potential," as Sarah experienced. Students may simply stop speaking, reading, or writing. They may choose easy educational tracks, or they may find themselves tracked at the discretion of school officials (Flanagan, 1993; Ogbu, 1994; Rose, 1990; Walsh, 1991). Some students may simply leave school, choosing one day, as Julia did when she left that final meeting, to go home and not return.

The problem of shutdown is, therefore, important and raises a number of questions:

- How can teachers avoid shutting out students?
- How can teachers become more aware of their role in causing or resisting shutdown in their students?
- What causes some people to resist shutting down?
- What are some of the social factors that contribute to shutting down?

Implications From the Research

The women in this study had literacy- and language-based memories from an early age and did not forget encounters in which literacy was related to failure. On the other hand, they remembered moments of school and literacy success by reciting poems, recalling memorable books, and sharing their writing. They all wanted to be active participants in learning and performance until these activities became associated with perfection or exclusivity; then some women shut down and relegated themselves to the "background." What are the implications of their shutting down? What can we as teachers learn from these stories?

I have included some examples of implications I deduced from these stories in the sections that follow. Although I realize that these implications are only a starting point for further research or classroom practice in relation to literacy, I think they are a good place to begin.

Shutdown Happens in a Variety of Ways

Silencing, social distancing, and nonreciprocity are interrelated and complex ways in which people shut down. Literacy and language use often are affected negatively when shutdown occurs. Those in positions of power should be aware of the subtle ways in which silencing, distancing, and nonreciprocity occur in well-intended human interactions. For example, Julia fled a meeting and made an excuse for her exit: As she perceived it, *terminology and piles of paper* clouded the meeting's purpose. Beverly and Sarah, who defined their backgrounds as affluent and middle- or upper middle class, suggested that a powerful responsibility to class status directed their use of literacy. Sarah refused to let anyone be privy to her writing, which might reveal misspelled words. Beverly avoided lengthy books in school and learned to hide her reading speed from her teachers. She later refused to join book clubs, which might reveal to her friends her inability to read quickly. Ella chose not to read aloud in her integrated high school for fear of not being accepted by white students.

Memory of Being Shut Out Is Powerful

In terms of literacy and language use, memories of arrogant perceptions affect one's willingness to risk being perceived arrogantly in future encounters with persons perceived as more educated or more correct. These memories can contribute to linguistic or literacy paralysis. Ella's recollections of entering a white high school are clear in her mind; she recalls a sense of "doom." So powerful are her memories that she did not want her children to experience the same feelings of being looked down on by others. Angel, too, had never forgotten the treatment of her teachers who looked at her as a child "on welfare." Beverly never forgot the lessons about grammatical correctness learned from her grandmother or the language used to define a person from an "unfortunate background."

Perceptions of Teachers Matter

Regardless of whether a teacher is perceived as arrogant, he or she often is perceived as "correct." This perception is powerful and can cause one who is not a master of standard English or perfect spelling to fear speaking or writing in front of the teacher. Both Ella and Beverly commented on their perceptions that I was "correct" and an "expert in grammar" because I was an English teacher. Sarah attributed her dislike and fear of writing to specific teachers, their red ink, and their insistence on not bending the rules, but she also remembered her college writing teacher who was more forgiving. The perceptions of teachers and mentors were salient in the minds of all the women, and the words of those kind, gentle teachers who believed in them and did not look down on them had been internalized. Ella, Angel, and Julia recalled the exact words of those who had motivated, loved, and believed in them.

Families Affect Shutdown

The research of Dahl and Freppon (1995) suggests that "The linked patterns of sense of self as reader/writer and persistence indicated the establishment of a 'disposition for learning' and provided evidence of learner ownership and a positive attitude toward literacy" (p. 70). A disposition for learning fostered at an early age seemed to help Angel and Edna resist shutting down when faced with arrogant perceptions. The following factors from the experiences of Angel and Edna seemed to contribute to this disposition: (1) strong and loving mentors who read in their presence and encouraged them to read and to express their own ideas about what they had read; (2) mentors who had high expectations for their academic success (Entwisle & Hayduck, 1988); (3) mentors who encouraged creative play and dramatic performance; (4) moderately structured (neither rigid nor authoritarian) educational, home, and church institutions; (5) exposure to a wide range of literary materials; and (6) exposure to women who took risks and did not fear imperfection.

Shutdown Is Not Always Absolute

The women who shut down more readily did not possess a strong disposition for learning; however, they continued to read and write privately. Although they feared revealing imperfection in using their literacy skills publicly (in seeking jobs requiring writing, in furthering their education, or in participating in community activities requiring reading), they did not stop reading and writing. These literate acts remained an outlet for expression; they did not consistently use literacy or language in a reflective or confident sense, perhaps because they did not have a safe outlet for expression and reflection. In the privacy of her own home, Beverly read big, thick books; in fact, all the women did. Frequently, they read books that were related to their spiritual or personal growth. Brodkey (1992) notes that materials of a religious nature are frequently not allowed in public schools, and yet this type of discourse is one with which many people are comfortable. Their writing was also of a personal, expressive nature. Perhaps teachers of literacy need to focus on teaching literate skills in conjunction with making sense of personal experiences (Chamblee, 1998; Gere, 1994). The institutional school structure, however, will have to be a safe place (Pratt, 1991).

Literacy Narratives Are Important

All the women who participated in this study described changes in literacy and language awareness, and several noted changes in literacy behaviors during the research period. Sarah began writing more and keeping a journal. Edna recalled memories during the interviews, which she was prompted to share through public speaking engagements. Ella created a new resumé. Julia continued to write. Beverly shared her transcripts with her family so that she could "tell" them her feelings.

Attitudes Can Be Examined

Teacher education programs should include courses that focus on teacher attitudes and arrogant perceptions. These courses may require student teachers to visit and work in communities different from those in which they live. Future literacy teachers should be made cognizant of literacy and language as it is used in the everyday life of their students (Cushman, 1996; McCaleb, 1994; Minter, Gere, & Keller-Cohen, 1995). The women in this study were able to analyze readily literacy in their lives and the power of literacy through the interview process, transcription review, and reflective dialogue. Teacher education programs could incorporate the same techniques.

A Discussion of Shutdown

In order for people to see themselves as literacy learners, they must be allowed to discuss their fears regarding language and perceptions of cultural correctness. They must have safe places in which to reflect on language and the transformations it undergoes in different contexts. In recalling their school experiences, Ella, Julia, Sarah, Beverly, and Angel did not remember being asked their opinions about their reading or to write anything other than essays and documented papers. Beverly and Sarah recalled books on how to write papers. The focus of writing seemed to be on correctness rather than opinion or reflection; the focus of reading seemed to be on speed and accuracy in word pronunciation rather than understanding or enjoyment.

What roles do teachers and educational institutions play in this complex process of shutting down and shutting out? What roles do they play in helping people resist shutting down and being shut out? The women in the stories frequently mentioned being "invited" or "encouraged" to be participants. Do we, as teachers, extend genuine invitations to become literacy learners, or do our perceptions of others become relational barriers to their success? Do teachers understand the complex and interrelated nature of silencing, social distancing, and nonreciprocity in relation to background differences?

The experiences of Julia highlight the interrelatedness of silencing, social distancing, and nonreciprocity in relation to persons in power. Julia was so thrilled when she was invited to participate in the meetings on governmental assistance that she bought a new outfit to wear. Her excitement waned, however, when she sensed no reciprocity for her knowledge and she realized that arrogance prevailed. She and those whom she represented were "cases" in the eyes of those in charge. Julia gladly accepted the invitation to be a discussion participant. However, she contends that a hierarchy is maintained by those in power to keep themselves employed. If they stopped being arrogant, their jobs and their "I'm-better-than-you" position would have to change. She lost *trust* in those in power, and she shut down.

Julia learned to be silenced at home and at school. In these environments, Julia had little opportunity to use "oral and written forms of language" (Belenky et al., 1986) as a reflective tool to make sense of her own ideas. Discussing reading, discussing writing, speaking, and listening—potentially nonthreatening reflective encounters between persons—did not occur at home or at school. These environments were structured authoritatively and, as an African American woman in the rural South in the mid-20th century, she did not feel free to speak. However, Julia possesses language tools and skills; she is literate by definition. She reads and writes today, but they are private activities, except at church, the one institution where she felt safe to express herself through music when she was a child.

Julia retreated from those in power whom she felt were using her into a world of silence where it was safe. She knows the liberating power of writing to express one's innermost thoughts. Her writing is a testimony to her belief in the power of literacy. Her poems and songs illustrate her belief that words can give meaning to emotion and experience. However, because of her race, education, and life circumstances, her literacy capital currently does not seem to give her enough power in U.S. society, but she is a woman of incredible faith who goes to work and church and participates in her community.

Fine (1992), in discussing silencing, expressed well what happened to Julia in her meetings with the "bigwigs": "Not naming, as a particular form of silencing, was accomplished creatively" (p. 123). Julia knew the topics that needed to be discussed were being ignored. The topics were being "named," but the facilitators "creatively" parked them. In Brodkey's (1990) work, the ABE students wrote about real situations in their lives (a friend's husband was murdered, and "a good man [who] would give you the shirt off of his back" was the killer). The white middle-class teachers did not know how to respond. To them the murder became "the problem." Renaming in such vague terms constitutes "a discursive retreat" that has the power to "reconstitute" the persons involved, according to Brodkey. The teachers, like the bigwigs, had the power to invite correspondence, but they too parked the real issues. Beverly recalled that she had "dropped" the conversation when an African American woman approached Beverly about her perceptions of "barriers" within a group to which they both belonged. Beverly admitted that she did not know how to discuss racial barriers. This subtly powerful manner of handling topics contributes to silencing and distancing but can also fuel anger. Julia noted in her interviews with me that she was not financially compensated for her time or input at the meetings to which she was invited. Interestingly, she did not see this as an issue until she read a newspaper article in which her ideas were attributed to a "man in power [who] had no knowledge" of the lives of the people to whom he was referring.

Is Julia correct in her observations? Do people in power *respect* others who have less than enough to help them learn and grow? In order to convey respect to Julia and to give her the "*boldness*" she so desperately wanted, the facilitators in charge of the meetings Julia described would have had to sacrifice their agenda and park their own topics. Freire (1993) believed that "To these professionals, it seems absurd to consider the necessity of respecting the 'view of the world' held by the people" (p. 137). These bigwigs were attempting to respect the people; however, they simply could not sacrifice their power enough to admit that they did not have knowledge of the issues from any point of view other than their own, according to Julia.

Although background differences contribute to moments of distrust, discomfort, and distancing, Angel suggested that simple arrogance stemming from these differences is one factor that drives people to shut down, or in her case, to "misbehave" because they sense that they are being shut out by someone who is "*stuffy*." Angel commented that some teachers are perceived as arrogant because they tend to look down on students and make them feel "not good enough." "They are stuffy; they turn up their noses." On the issue of trust, I asked her at the end of our interviews why she agreed to participate in this study with me. She laughed and responded quickly, "I sized you up and looked right into the window of your soul. I can tell the difference between whether a person has a genuine love for people or if they have the mentality of 'What can you do for me now?' I can decide between those types of people. I'm not comfortable around them because I always feel like I have to be on guard, and then I don't want to be there."

Do some educators use students to meet enrollment or grading quotas, to get grants, or to keep themselves employed? Are some educators taking instead of giving? Sacrificing these motives in the world of education might create a situation in which everyone could grow.

Sarah's family had many material benefits, and she was expected to go to college. She was always in the "college-bound group," which she concluded was determined by the income level and social class of parents. College was "*just the next phase of life*" for an upper-middle-class white child in her southern town. Sarah expressed incredible frustration, however, at being tracked in this manner all her life. Sarah's words are worth repeating: "My early models in *how to live life* gave me the impression that there was one way to do things, only one way, and that things had to be done *perfectly*, that *rigidity* was the way things had to be accomplished."

Like Julia, Sarah had often shut down. She recalled as a little girl trying to win the praise of her parents by writing and performing; however, she received no praise for creative efforts or risk taking. Band became an outlet for her, but she noted that to this day she cannot "go outside and ad lib." She was taught early in life—in home, school, and church—that she must work to her potential and that she must memorize and learn material by rote. She learned that to take risks and to express herself creatively were dangerous practices and might subject her to failure or imperfection. When she received no praise for creative efforts, she stated, "I felt *shutdown, and I don't go back there. And the safe areas got fewer and fewer as time went on.*" Sarah retreated into the safe world of books, but she avoids writing to this day, for a misspelled word or a grammatical error would reveal her imperfection. She knew the racial and class boundaries of her town. She knew that she must distance herself from the poor African Americans and whites who lived in one area of town, or she would not "feed the self-perceptions" of her peer group. She is now a woman desperate to be free, no longer "a shell walking around day-by-day." She wants to be part of institutions that are flexible and tolerant of imperfection. She wants to know "healthy people who don't have to pretend to be other than who they are."

Sarah's feelings about cultural perfection tormented her and strongly affected her need to shut down—for fear of being shut out or not meeting the expectations of those in power. She was trapped by the same arrogant perceptions of cultural correctness and capital that caused Ella to believe that she was too old to fix.

Shutting Out People

Maria Lugones's (1987) words are worth repeating: "To the extent that we learn to perceive others arrogantly or come to see them only as products of arrogant perception and continue to perceive them that way, we fail to identify with them—fail to love them" (p. 4). Ella and Julia might ask, If we're all God's children, why would anybody think that he or she is superior to anybody else? We're human beings; we're all people. I'm pretty sure that, if he could, my father would agree with them.

Human beings are often insecure. Their self-esteem is boosted by what Ella described as "degrees, titles—something." They desperately want to be in charge of someone or something to boost their own self-importance. They like the comfort and safety of the circles and cliques mentioned by Beverly and Sarah. Sarah observed these cliques, of which she never felt a part: "Women are selected for admittance because they will feed the self-perceptions of the other women in the group. Those who do not fit this perception are excluded." And those who are excluded feel hurt, for in Ella's words, their exclusion has just revealed "*who [they] are and where [they] are from*" or, according to Beverly, "*their background or way of doing things.*"

Are some elements of one's background better than others? Obviously, as Edna was taught, some clothes are finer, some schools are better. Ella, too, saw clearly that the white children's school building, so big and beautiful, and the white children's books, neither ragged nor torn, were better than her school with the outhouse and the hand-me-down books. Some things are better than others. Both Ella and Edna grew up in the rural South, and both learned this lesson by observing their lives in contrast to the lives of others. Edna admonished us, regardless of our station, to have some manners and make people feel *comfortable*. Make time to know what people think and feel. *Just love them.*

In order to exhibit these manners to which Edna is referring, we would have to be so comfortable with ourselves that we would not feel any need to be anything other than ourselves in the presence of others, the kind of people for whom Sarah is so desperately looking. I do not think that just loving people is done easily; it involves risk. It involves getting close enough to other people to learn about their backgrounds and experiences, which may not neatly mirror our own. We may be afraid of what we see, or we may not approve of it. To get close enough to understand how people feel means that we cannot just shut them out or, in Beverly's words, "cut them off." We have to invite them to talk and reciprocate by acknowledging their named experiences and giving credit to their vocabulary. We must neither park their topics nor signal a discursive retreat. If we get close enough to see into their hearts, we may at least come to understand and respect their views. We may even discover why the child wrote about killing his teacher, the inappropriate topic that so disturbed Edna.

Many people from Christian and other religious backgrounds are taught to love others. They also, as exhibited by the stories of Sarah, Beverly, and Edna, are taught to dress, act, and speak in a certain manner based on class expectations and the material benefits to be derived from existence in a perceived social class. Edna herself, though poor, "observed and did exactly" as store officials did. Her mother refused to allow her children to associate with "vulgar people—coarse, vulgar people who didn't read and didn't go to church." Sarah and Beverly were expected to go to college and to live a certain way based on their parents' income and educational level. Beverly first disappointed her father by not reading well and then by dropping out of college. She also defied her grandmother by marrying someone from a blue-collar background, someone whose "grammar was noticeable." There was a price to pay for just loving someone whose background was different. Beverly bravely took risks and still takes risks, but her early lessons about correctness are rooted deeply.

In addition to being trained in awareness of class differences, sometimes people are trained simultaneously to perceive arrogantly those who are different. Beverly was taught that people from blue-collar backgrounds talked differently. She admitted that growing up

97

she had, in fact, been quite insulated from knowing people who were poor or of different races. Edna seems to have been taught to distance herself or shut out those whose *moral* behavior was unacceptable or "vulgar"—moral behavior correlated with the ability to read and to be well educated. These lessons about class are often tied to the American myth of individualism: Those who choose to behave in a certain manner will succeed or, in Sarah's words, "climb the ladder of success." Ogbu (1994) noted, however, that these beliefs often "form a screen" that prevents those in positions of power from analyzing "symbolic and relational barriers" and responses (p. 282). Too often, he suggests, we focus our attempts to achieve equality on attacking "instrumental barriers," tangible elements of existence, such as housing, jobs, and educational test performance. However, we must work to find ways to become aware of relational barriers and our responses. Our fear of difference, our own insecurities, and our arrogant perceptions of others may be factors influencing the sense of acceptance that so many people desire in order that they may grow in self-confidence and self-respect.

Often during the internal struggle to reconcile the idea of loving all people with the idea of becoming a correct person and meshing nicely with class expectations and those insidious arrogant perceptions, people in power simply find it easier to shut out people from different backgrounds who are not correct. Beverly admitted that having shut out people now made her feel *terrible*, but that she was aware, through our discussions, that she had excluded people—"cut them off"—based on their background and race.

How do the people feel who are shut out? Ella said that she felt like she was *too old to fix*; that she was not correct, that people looked at her like a *let-down*. Julia said that she *shut down like a light switch*, that she had *always been afraid of making a mistake*, and that she *had felt like she was nobody*.

It is not only difficult to love others. It is difficult to love oneself at times if one must always attempt to be what others expect and their love or approval seems to be a condition of meeting those correct expectations. As Sarah tried to become what those in the middle-class expected, she eventually became a *shell walking around day-by-day, a struggling, unhappy person*. Beverly had trouble feeling free to love others. She always felt like she was in a role that suggested that she was better than others—a role dictating her performance and necessitating that any inadequacies be hidden. Both Beverly and Sarah are working now to be free to accept themselves and others.

To reconcile humanitarian or religious beliefs about loving others, people can love those from dissimilar backgrounds safely and at a distance through charitable or dutiful acts, and the moral tension can be reconciled without personal contact. Those who passed down used books to the African American students in Ella's school perceived their acts as charitable and loving, while maintaining their distance. However, when the schools were desegregated, the distance was observed by Ella as the white kids sitting on one side of the classroom and the African Americans kids sitting on the other side. Julia saw the lives of those not in power neatly sorted in folders being read in an office far from where they live. Lives handled in this distant and charitable manner creates work for the bigwigs. Sarah was surrounded by people intent on teaching her a list of "thou shall nots." In school, church, and her home, she recalled no affirmation or love, only guilt production. Lessons were learned using rote drill and memorization, dutifully at a distance.

Brodkey (1990) made a critical point: The teachers who "distanced and alienated" themselves are not "ogres." Neither are many people who are uncomfortable crossing into other worlds or are uncomfortable with getting to know other people. Often they do not know how to begin. Beverly did not know, because she had never examined the barriers that contribute to the belief system of white, middle-class experience or her own responses. Like myself and many others, she had not considered the responses of those not privy to this system.

Those human beings in power are shaped by their own experiences. They may not understand poverty or a world in which going to college is a dream rather than an expectation. They may believe that going outside their own circle of friends risks exclusion if they tarnish the self-perception of the circle, as Sarah suggested. Those in power are also part of institutions that have historically sanctioned what Brodkey terms "discursive hegemony." Teachers are comfortable teaching literacy skills in the safety of a vacuum. For example, essays on Russian literature are safe, but essays by 10-year-olds on how to murder their teachers are not. Perhaps teachers think if the topics are controlled and correct, then the students and their problems will magically self-correct or disappear.

What if a student decides that he or she is too old to fix or that his or her background cannot be made *correct*? The student may shut down, for in essence the student has sensed being shut out—because the student may not feel loved or accepted. Julia and Ella, based on their interpretations of their early religious lessons, see this shutting out as wrong. To them love is defined in the New Testament as neither arrogant nor conditional.

Conditional love or acceptance and arrogance seem to thrive in rigidly structured institutions, in authoritarian homes, schools, and churches that are intolerant or fearful of difference. Such institutions will not tolerate rule bending, flights of fancy, or loving persons from a different background—unless they magically remake themselves and immediately acquire a proper background and, according to Edna, exposure to "a very outstanding background knowledge." Edna had mentors willing to expose her to "knowing finer things," and she lived in a socioeconomically diverse neighborhood that allowed for this *exposure*. She could see other worlds—of literature, music, and opportunity—on her own street. She felt loved in her own home and was encouraged to take risks and voice her opinions.

Those in power in rigidly structured institutions often are not willing to encourage questioning or empowering attitudes about learning. They will encourage passivity and submission and the "rote memorization" that Sarah recalled. They will teach "guilt-production instead of affirmation" to preserve the status quo and to create "proper" Sarahs.

Those in power in schools may shut out students whom they arrogantly perceive and label according to social class. Even as a child, Angel sensed the power of class perceptions. As early as first grade, Angel perceived that her teachers disliked her because her mother was on welfare. However, encouraged by her mother never to give up, Angel always completed her homework and prepared her lessons. Angel, therefore, defied stereotypical perceptions and refused to be shut out. She rebelled by misbehaving until her third-grade teacher graded her on her "work" and encouraged her to excel academically.

Every day people are shut out in intersecting and complex ways. We shut out people because of our own fear and insecurity. We fear being excluded from our circle of friends, so we exclude those who may speak, look, or dress differently. Through the important "shaping" institutions of schools, and churches, we perpetuate this exclusionary process. To help us accomplish this unpleasant and uncomfortable work, we use certain strategies, structuring devices, and literacy tools and practices to maintain the boundaries.

Many neighborhoods have become exclusionary and homogeneous along socioeconomic lines. Poor children have little exposure to other worlds of possibility because they do not have the money for travel and computers. The wealthy neighbors who loaned their classics to Edna now have moved and insulated themselves in affluent suburbs. We often teach children to become passive learners, especially those not labeled gifted and talented; we often teach shutting down. We park uncomfortable topics and control what is read, discussed, and written. Those in power within institutions often hire those from similar backgrounds to perpetuate and not threaten the desired self-image.

Resisting Shutdown

I hope we all become more aware of our own arrogant perceptions and understand their influence in the lives of those we touch. As teachers we need to be aware that our perceptions do influence those who are "shaped" by us. We also need to understand factors that may contribute to one's resistance to feeling shut out and refusal to be shut down when confronted with the arrogant perceptions of others.

All of the women in this study had resisted being shut down in some way. Some were motivated to fight for their children, some for themselves. I believe that each woman wants to be heard and respected, to possess, as Julia said, a "*boldness*" like Angel and Edna, both of whom recalled instances in which they believed themselves to be the objects of arrogant perception. Both women were hurt by the encounters, but they refused to let experiences negatively affect their participation in educational or religious pursuits. They also refused to let these experiences negatively affect their self-perceptions or feelings of self-worth.

Both Angel and Edna were reared by strong, independent women who taught them confidence and an understanding of literacy *before they began school.* They possessed what Dahl and Freppon (1995) describe as "literate behaviors" as distinguished from "literate skills."

> Literacy skills are the concepts and behaviors that learners use as they read and write. They are elements of proficient reading and writing that are taught and practiced in most school-based settings. Literate behaviors are somewhat broader; they include learners reflecting on their own literate activity and using oral language to interact with written language by reacting to a story, explaining a piece of writing, or describing a favorite book to another person (Heath & Hoffman, 1986). Literate behaviors also include taking on the tasks of reading and writing, valuing one's own experience and personal language and connecting them with written language, and communicating about written language experiences. (p. 71)

Perhaps having a disposition for learning and having literate behaviors would influence one's ability to better resist shutting down in language- and literacy-related practices. Angel and Edna saw their mothers read at home, and both mothers read to their children. They used reading and writing skills in play and were encouraged to recite, perform, and express themselves creatively. Women who frequently shut down—who retreated into a world of silence or who distanced themselves from those perceived as more educated or more powerful—did not seem to possess literate behaviors to the same degree. Both Angel and Edna have a disposition for learning and are modeling that attitude to their own children and grandchildren. In fact, both women used the same term in describing their beliefs about teaching children: In order for children to learn, one should do "whatever it takes for kids to get it."

Although Ella, Julia, Beverly, and Sarah resisted shutting down at various times in their lives, their resistance was not as consistent. Julia, Beverly, and Sarah had been "shaped" in authoritarian and male-dominated institutions. At least for Ella, Julia, and Beverly, church was a safe place where certain kinds of expression by women were permitted. Julia and Sarah did not recall any particularly encouraging, loving female mentors and role models during their early years. These women had been taught in different ways that school literacy correlated with correct performance and perfection, and rote memorization. Unfortunately, school literacy then became enmeshed with one's race and social class and privilege—the creation of a "correct" person. One had to read, write, and speak *correctly*, or one would reveal one's *background*, and the fear of being found less-than-correct seemed to paralyze, at times, all of these women. Reading and writing were safely decontextualized in school, and they were not used for connection with life, enjoyment, or personal expression. To use reading and writing in this manner was and still is a risk. These women, in some ways, have passive dispositions about learning. Yet, each has responded positively when invited to speak or to perform. Each woman has used literacy in the form of reading or journal, letter, and poetry writing as a lifeline to expression. Each woman seemed to enjoy speaking in this study and reflecting on her experiences and ideas.

Ella, Julia, Angel, and Edna each had at least one teacher or mentor who had "loved" them and had faith in them. These mentors invited them to participate in learning; they encouraged them. They also had high expectations, but they resisted rigidity. Although Julia recalled no encouraging teachers, she eventually had a mentor who gave her a job and told her that she could do the work. These teachers and mentors did not shut out anyone because of race, class, or background (Alexander, Entwisle, & Thompson, 1987). Each one *just loved* her students and had faith in them; they were not distanced by arrogant perceptions. They handed these women a lifeline to expression— through literacy—and to possible "*boldness*."

Conclusion

Although I am sure that temperament or genetic predisposition to behaviors and responses affects one's feelings of being shut out or perceived arrogantly, it was not my intent in this research to analyze temperament. I believe that each woman interviewed, regardless of temperament, background, or context, expressed a need to have her thoughts named and respected. Each recognized that literacy is a means to this end. In our debates about literacy and literacy pedagogy, I think we have overlooked an obvious and needed point: Human thought and knowledge change constantly; however, human feeling basically remains constant across time and cultures (Cahill, 1995). Human beings learn differently and have different strengths and weaknesses, but human feeling is a constant.

Perhaps Edna informed us as to what we may have forgotten about teaching reading, writing, or a new language: Maybe we do have to make time to know what people think and feel. Maybe we do have to *just love them*. Arrogant perceptions, however, may make these tasks more difficult than they should be. Sometimes we are so arrogant about the rightness of our philosophical views that we forget the human beings at the heart of our academic battles. I am sure that we can teach people to read and to write and to use rules for standard English if we first accept their language and literacy, elements that are part of their being.

Children make sense of literacy and language at an early age (Dahl & Freppon, 1995; Wolfram & Christian, 1993). This understanding is tied not only to factors of background, but also to perceptions of those with whom they are engaged. If early encounters are somehow tainted by sensed arrogance or extreme rigidity, children may be prone to shut down in relation to literacy and language use in the future.

For all our pedagogical and theoretical debates, students will continue to shut down and leave schools unless we who teach sacrifice our arrogant perceptions about background and literacy capital. We must get to know the students we teach and *just love them*, or they may never be comfortable reading, writing, or speaking in our presence, acts that they may perceive as intimidating. James C. Raymond (1982) said quite well that "The world of high literacy in this country is not a huge melting pot in which all but a few recalcitrant minorities have been purified of their linguistic quirks. It is a relatively small teakettle with a very powerful whistle" (p. 8). It is powerful—so powerful that it frightens some people into silence. I do not suggest giving up standard conventions—most of the students whom I teach desperately want to master them. However, I suggest recognizing the intimidating power of literacy and the arrogance that can accompany it. Those of us in power by virtue of race, education, or background need to assess and analyze how we feel about those we teach. If any arrogant perceptions or barriers are found hiding in our hearts, I suggest we begin to bring them into the light and face them. We need to sacrifice them in order for others to grow.

ℐotes

Language, Literacy, and Living: An Introduction

1. (p. 1) I thank Dr. Barbara Ash of Auburn University for fine-tuning my thinking and alerting me to "shutting out" as a concept worthy of exploration and tied to my research.

2. (p. 3) Mary Soliday (1994) discusses the importance of literacy narratives as a way for people "to explore the profound cultural force language exerts in their everyday lives" (p. 511). She defines literacy narratives as the "sites of self-translation where writers can articulate the meanings and the consequences of their passages between language worlds" (p. 511).

Chapter 2: Conducting a Literacy Enthnography: Hearing How People Feel

1. (p. 23) Again, my thanks to Dr. Barbara Ash of Auburn University who introduced the word "judgment" to our dialogue regarding issues in qualitative research. Her critical and insightful reading of my manuscripts always raised new issues.

Guiding Questions for Interview One: Life Circumstances

Note: *If any items are too sensitive, do not feel compelled to answer. We'll just go to the next question and talk about something else.*

1. When and where were you born?
2. Describe where you lived while growing up.
   a. Tell me about your house and neighborhood.
   b. Describe your school and community.
3. Tell me about your family when you were growing up.
   a. What did your parents do for a living?
   b. How would you describe the educational level of your parents?
   c. How would you describe the economic conditions of your family?
   d. Did you have to work? If so, tell me about it.
   e. Can you recall a time when you were made to feel bad about your circumstances or your family? What prompted it? Was it in any way related to language, how you spoke?
   f. Can you recall a time when you were proud of your family? What prompted it?
4. Tell me about where you live now.
   a. Describe your house and your neighborhood.
   b. Describe the school your children attend.
   c. What kinds of things do you do in your community?
   d. Where do you shop?

5. Describe your family now.

    a. Are you married?

    b. Do you have children? Tell me about them.

    c. How would you describe the economic conditions of your family?

    d. Do you or your husband work? If so, tell me about your jobs.

    e. Do you like what you do? Explain.

    f. Describe your education. Tell me about your happiest memory of school. Tell me about your unhappiest memory of school.

6. List for me all the roles you have in life.

7. In your adult life, can you recall an experience during which you felt bad about your life circumstances?

8. In your adult life, can you recall an experience during which you felt good about your life circumstances?

9. What is one thing that you wish you could do or could have done in life?

    a. What do you think prevented you from accomplishing it?

10. What is your greatest accomplishment or source of pride in your life?

    a. Did anyone or anything, in particular, help you?

11. What is your happiest memory?

12. What is your unhappiest memory?

Guiding Questions for Interview Two: Reading, Writing, and Performance in the Context of Home and Family

1. Tell me who taught you to read.

2. What do you remember about reading in your family when you were growing up?

    a. Did anyone, in particular, read a lot or read aloud to you or your siblings?

    b. What did your parents tell you about learning to read?

3. Tell me about books and magazines and newspapers in your house.

4. Did you ever play school or church or use reading when you played with other children?

5. Tell me about reading in your home now.

    a. When does reading take place in your home?

    b. Do you have a lot of books, magazines, and newspapers?

    c. Do you read to your children or in front of them?

    d. What do you read? Is it for pleasure?

    e. Has anything you have ever read at home made a difference in your life? Explain.

6. How about writing? What are your first memories of writing at home?

7. Did you ever keep a diary? Tell me about it.

8. Do you write at home now? If so, what?

9. Do your children write at home? If so when and what?

10. Do you write letters?

11. How is writing important in your life?

12. Tell me about any times that you and your family read aloud, sang, or performed at home.

13. Were you ever embarrassed when reading at home? Tell me about the incident.

14. Were you ever proud of reading something at home? Tell me about it.

15. Did you ever feel funny, embarrassed, or put down about your writing at home? Tell me about it.

16. Do you recall a moment of pride regarding something that you wrote at home? Tell me about it.

17. At home, did you ever speak, read, or share written work and no one responded to you? Tell me about this and how it made you feel.

18. Has anything you have ever read, written, or performed at home had an impact in your life? Explain.

19. Who were the "performers" in your family?
   a. What do you think contributed to them becoming "performers"?
   b. How did you feel about their "performances"?

Guiding Questions for Interview Three: Reading, Writing, and Performance in the Context of School

1. Tell me about your earliest memories of reading in school.

2. How did you feel about reading aloud?

3. Tell me about an embarrassing or disappointing moment in reading at school—a moment that sticks in your mind.

4. Tell me about a moment of excitement or pride in reading at school.

5. Tell me about your reading teachers.

6. Tell me about the kinds of books you read in school.
   a. What were your impressions of these books?
   b. Tell me about any problems you had reading these books.
   c. Did you connect with the stories or materials read? If so, how?
   d. What advice would you have for teachers of reading?

7. How do you use reading in your life now?
   a. Was what you did in school practical?
   b. Were any of the books you read in school important in your life? What were they? How have they been important?

8. Tell me about your earliest memories of writing at school.

9. How did you feel about writing at school?
   a. Were you confident about writing?
   b. Were you comfortable about showing your writing to teachers or to others?

10. Tell me about an embarrassing or disappointing moment in writing at school—a moment that sticks in your mind.

11. Tell me about a moment of excitement or pride in writing at school.

12. Tell me about the kinds of writing you did in school.
    a. What were your impressions of these assignments?
    b. Tell me about any problems you had with the assignments.
    c. Describe your writing teachers.
    d. What advice would you have for teachers of writing?

13. How do you use writing in your life now?
    a. Was what you did in school helpful?
    b. Has anything you wrote in school ever been important in your life? What was it? How was it important?

14. Describe any instances of performing in school.
    a. Are they pleasant memories?
    b. If so, why?
    c. If unpleasant, why?
    d. Was the performance important in your life in any way? Explain.

15. Did you ever want to perform at school and not get the chance?
    a. Describe the situation.
    b. Why do you think you didn't get to perform?

16. What kind of people "performed" at school?

17. Did you go to college? Did you dream of college? Tell me about it.

Guiding Questions for Interview Four: Reading, Writing, and Performance in the Context of Church

1. As a child growing up, did you attend church? Describe the church.

2. Did you read at church? If so, tell me about what you read.
    a. Did you read silently, or were you read to?
    b. Did you enjoy or like the stories or materials?
    c. Did they connect with you?

3. Did you ever feel proud of reading at church?

4. Did you ever feel embarrassed while reading at church?

5. How about now? Describe your current church.

6. Do you read at church? If so, tell me about what you read.
    a. Do you read silently, or are you read to?
    b. Do you enjoy or like the stories or materials?
    c. Do they connect with you? If so, how?

7. Do you ever feel proud of reading at church now?

8. Do you ever feel embarrassed while reading at church now?

9. How does reading at church differ from reading at school or at home?

10. How is what you read in church important in your life?

11. Did you ever have to write at church when growing up? Tell me about it.

12. Did you ever feel proud of writing at church?

13. Did you ever feel embarrassed while writing at church?

14. How about now? Describe your current church.

15. Do you write at church now? If so, tell me about what you write.
    a. Do you enjoy the writing? Why?

16. Do you ever feel proud of writing at church now?

17. Do you ever feel embarrassed while writing at church now?

18. How does writing at church differ from writing at school or at home?

19. In what ways is this writing important in your life?

20. Tell me about performing at church when you were a child.

21. How did performing make you feel?

22. Were you ever left out and how did that make you feel?

23. Tell me about performing at church now.

24. How does it make you feel?

25. What would you describe as your proudest moment of performance at church and why?

26. What would you describe as your most embarrassing moment of performance at church and why?

27. What kind of people get to "perform" at church?

Guiding Questions for Evaluating the Research Experience

1. Describe your feelings and thoughts about the research process we've gone through and the time we have spent together talking.

2. Was there a time when you felt that I didn't understand you and that someone else might have?

3. If our backgrounds were the same, do you think that I might have understood your points better?

4. Have you experienced any changes in your life as a result of this research? Tell me about them.

Based on Taylor, J., Gilligan, C., & Sullivan, A.M. (1995). *Between voice and silence*. Cambridge, MA: Harvard University Press.

References

Alexander, K.L., Entwisle, D.R., & Thompson, M.S. (1987, October). School performance, status relations, and the structure of sentiment: Bringing the teacher back in. *American Sociological Review, 52,* 665–682.

Atwell, N. (1987). *In the middle: Writing, reading and learning with adolescents.* Portsmouth, NH: Boynton/Cook.

Baldwin, J. (1963). *The fire next time.* New York: Random.

Belenky, M.F., Clinchy, B.M., Goldberger, N.R., & Tarule, J.M. (1986). *Women's ways of knowing.* New York: Basic Books.

Bernstein, B. (1971). *Class codes and control: Theoretical studies towards a sociology of language* (Vol. 1). London: Routledge & Kegan Paul.

Bleich, D. (1988). *The double perspective.* New York: Oxford University Press.

Brandt, D. (1990). *Literacy as involvement: The acts of writers, readers, and texts.* Carbondale, IL: Southern Illinois University Press.

Brandt, D. (1995, October). Accumulating literacy: Writing and learning to write in the twentieth century. *College English, 57,* 649–668.

Brodkey, L. (1990, February). On the subjects of class and gender in "the literacy letters." In R.L. Graves (Ed.), *Rhetoric and composition* (pp. 279–295). Portsmouth, NH: Boynton/Cook.

Brodkey, L. (1992). Articulating poststructural theory in research on literacy. In R. Beach, J. Green, M. Kamil, & T. Shanahan (Eds.), *Multidisciplinary perspectives on literacy research* (pp. 293–318). Urbana, IL: National Conference on Research in English and National Council of Teachers of English.

Cahill, T. (1995). *How the Irish saved civilization.* New York: Bantam, Doubleday, Dell.

Chamblee, C.M. (1998, April). Bringing life to reading and writing for at-risk college students. *Journal of Adolescent & Adult Literacy, 41,* 532–537.

Cushman, E. (1996, February). The rhetorician as an agent of social change. *College Composition and Communication, 47,* 7–28.

Dahl, K.L., & Freppon, P.A. (1995). A comparison of innercity children's interpretations of reading and writing instruction in the early grades in skills-based and whole language classrooms. *Reading Research Quarterly, 30,* 50–74.

Denzin, N.K. (1978). *The research act: A theoretical introduction to sociological methods.* New York: McGraw-Hill.

Elsasser N., & Irvine, P. (1992). Literacy as commodity: Redistributing the goods. *Journal of Education, 174,* 26–40.

Entwisle, D.R., & Hayduk, L.A. (1988, July). Lasting effects of elementary school. *Sociology of Education, 61,* 147–159.

Fine, M. (1992). *Disruptive voices.* Ann Arbor, MI: University of Michigan Press.

Flanagan, C. (1993). Gender and social class: Intersecting issues in women's achievement. *Educational Psychologist, 28,* 357–378.

Freire, P. (1993). *Pedagogy of the oppressed.* New York: Continuum.

Gaines, Ernest J. (1993). *A lesson before dying.* New York: Knopf.

Gere, A.R. (1994, February). Kitchen tables and rented rooms: The extracurriculum of composition. *College Composition and Communication, 45,* 75–92.

Golding, William. (1959). *Lord of the flies.* New York: Berkley/Putnam.

Heath, S.B. (1983). *Ways with words.* New York: Cambridge University Press.

Heath, S.B., & Branscombe, A. (1985). "Intelligent writing" in an audience community: Teacher, students, and researcher. In S.W. Freedman (Ed.), *The acquisition of written language* (pp. 3–32). Norwood, NJ: Ablex.

Heath, S.B., & Hoffman, D.M. (1986). *Inside learners: Interactive reading in the elementary classroom* [Videotape]. Palo Alto, CA: Stanford University.

Hourigan, M.M. (1994). *Literacy as social exchange.* Albany, NY: State University of New York Press.

Labov, W. (1972). *Language in the inner city.* Philadelphia, PA: University of Pennsylvania Press

LeCompte, M.D. (1993). A framework for hearing silence: What does telling stories mean when we are supposed to be doing science? In D. McLaughlin & W.G. Tierney (Eds.), *Naming silenced lives* (pp. 9–27). New York: Routledge.

LeCompte, M.D., & Preissle, J. (1993). *Ethnography and qualitative design in educational research.* San Diego, CA: Academic Press.

Lee, Harper. (1988). *To kill a mockingbird.* New York: Time/Warner.

Lubeck, S. (1988). Nested contexts. In L. Weis (Ed.), *Class, race, and gender in American education* (pp. 43–62). Albany, NY: State University of New York Press.

Lugones, M. (1987). Playfulness, "world"-travelling, and loving perception. *Hypatia, 2,* 3–19.

McCaleb, S.P. (1994). *Building communities of learners.* New York: St. Martin's Press.

McCall, N. (1994). *Makes me wanna holler.* New York: Vintage Books.

McLaren, P. (1992). Literacy research and the postmodern turn: Cautions from the margins. In R. Beach, J. Green, M. Kamil, T. Shanahan (Eds.), *Multidisciplinary perspectives on literacy research* (pp. 319–339). Urbana, IL: National Conference on Research in English and National Council of Teachers of English.

Minter, D.W., Gere, A.R., & Keller-Cohen, D. (1995, October). Learning literacies. *College English, 57,* 669–687.

Moss, B.J. (Ed.). (1994). *Literacy across communities.* Cresskill, NJ: Hampton Press.

Ogbu, J. (1987). Variability in minority school performance: A problem in search of an explanation. *Anthropology and Education Quarterly, 18,* 312–382.

Ogbu, J. (1991). Cultural diversity and school experience. In C. Walsh (Ed.), *Literacy as praxis* (pp. 25–50). Norwood, NJ: Ablex.

Ogbu, J. (1994). Racial stratification and education in the United States: Why inequality persists. *Teachers College Record, 96,* 264–298.

Pratt, M.L. (1991). Arts of the contact zone. *Profession 91,* 33–40.

Raymond, J.C. (Ed.). (1982). *Literacy as a human problem.* University, AL: University of Alabama Press.

Rockhill, K. (1993). Gender, language, and the politics of literacy. In B. Street (Ed.), *Cross-cultural approaches to literacy* (pp. 156–175). Cambridge, UK: Cambridge University Press.

Rose, M. (1990). *Lives on the boundary.* New York: Penguin.

Royster, J. (1996, February). When the first voice you hear is not your own. *College Composition and Communication, 47,* 29–40.

Scribner, S., & Cole, M. (1981). *The psychology of literacy.* Cambridge, MA: Harvard University Press.

Shaughnessy, M. (1977). *Errors and expectations.* New York: Oxford University Press.

Sigel, I.E., & Cocking, R.R. (1977). *Cognitive development from childhood to adolescence: A constructivist perspective.* New York: Holt, Rinehart & Winston.

Snow, C.E., Barnes, W.S., Chandler, J., Goodman, I.F., & Hemphill, L. (1991). *Unfulfilled expectations.* Cambridge, MA: Harvard University Press.

Soliday, M. (1994, September). Translating self and difference through literacy narratives. *College English, 56,* 511–526.

Spellmeyer, K. (1993, March). "Too little care": Language, politics, and embodiment in the life-world. *College English, 55,* 265–283.

Spellmeyer, K. (1996, December). After theory: From textuality to attunement with the world. *College English, 58,* 893–913.

Stanback, M. (1988, Spring). What makes scholarship about black women and communication feminist communication scholarship? *Women's Studies in Communication, 11,* 28–31.

Street, B. (Ed.). (1993). *Cross-cultural approaches to literacy.* Cambridge, UK: Cambridge University Press.

Stuckey, J.E. (1991). *The violence of literacy.* Portsmouth, NH: Boynton/Cook.

Taylor, D. (1983). *Family literacy.* Exeter, NH: Heinemann.

Taylor, J., Gilligan, C., & Sullivan, A.M. (1995). *Between voice and silence.* Cambridge, MA: Harvard University Press.

Walsh, C.E. (1991). Literacy as praxis: A framework and an introduction. In C.E. Walsh (Ed.), *Literacy as praxis: Culture, language, and pedagogy* (pp. 1–22). Norwood, NJ: Ablex.

Wolfram, W., & Christian, D. (1993). Dialect differences and education. In D. Sheridan (Ed.), *Teaching secondary English* (pp. 223–232).White Plains, NY: Longman.

Zinsser, C. (1986). For the Bible tells me so: Teaching children in a fundamentalist church. In B.B. Schieffelin & P. Gilmore (Eds.), *The acquisition of literacy: Ethnographic perspectives* (pp. 55–71). Norwood, NJ: Ablex.

Author Index

Note: An *n* following an index entry indicates that the citation may be found in Endnotes.

I–K

Irvine, P., 3, 116
Keller-Cohen, D., 92, 117

L

Labov, W., 3, 116
LeCompte, M.D., 15, 23, 116
Lubeck, S., 17, 116
Lugones, M., 3, 13, 18, 96, 116

M

McCaleb, S.P., 92, 116
McCall, N., 72, 117
McLaren, P., 87, 117
Minter, D.W., 92, 117
Moss, B.J., 15, 16, 117

O–P

Ogbu, J., 3, 88, 98, 117
Pratt, M.L., 32, 91, 117
Preissle, J., 23, 116

R

Raymond, J.C., 2, 104, 117
Rockhill, K., 3, 17, 117

Rose, M., 3, 12, 13, 15, 26, 74, 88, 117
Royster, J., 16, 117

S

Scribner, S., 6, 117
Shaughnessy, M., 2, 15, 117
Sigel, I.E., 6, 117
Snow, C.E., 17, 117
Soliday, M., 105n. 2; 117
Spellmeyer, K., 13, 15, 18, 88, 117
Stanback, M., 30, 41, 118
Street, B., 4, 16, 20, 118
Stuckey, J.E., 64, 118
Sullivan, A.M., 22, 114, 118

T

Tarule, J.M., 5, 115
Taylor, D., 3, 15, 118
Taylor, J., 22, 114, 118
Thompson, M.S., 103, 115

W–Z

Walsh, C.E., 2, 88, 118
Wolfram, W., 104, 118
Zinsser, C., 59, 118

Subject Index

Note: An *n* following an index entry indicates that the citation may be found in Endnotes.

McCall's, 41
McMillan, Terry, 72
Metacognitive ability, 1
Millay, Edna St. Vincent, 74
Minorities, 30

N

Narratives, 91, 105*n*. 2
Norris, Kathleen, 80

O–P

Oral lessons, 30–31, 40
Performance, 26
Performance at church: Angel's story, 68; Beverly's story, 50–51; Ella's story, 32, 33; guiding questions for, 112–113; Julia's story, 38; Sarah's story, 59–60
Performance at home: Beverly's story, 49; guiding questions for, 108–109; Sarah's story, 58
Performance at school: Angel's story, 68–69, 71, 73–74; Beverly's story, 52; Ella's story, 33, 34–35; guiding questions for, 110–111; Sarah's story, 58, 62
Power-fullness, 17, 24

Q–R

Questions: for evaluating research experience, 114; for interviews, 106–107, 108–109, 110–111, 112–113
"Race pride", 71
Racial diversity, 2–3
The Rainmaker (Grisham), 48
Rand, Ayn, 80
Reader's Digest, 48
Reading: book reports, 71; books, 34, 56, 80; Great Books program, 83; Little Golden Books, 56; teaching, 52–53, 67
Reading at church: Angel's story, 68; Beverly's story, 50–51; Ella's story, 29, 32; guiding questions for, 112–113; Sarah's story, 59, 60
Reading at home: Angel's story, 67, 72, 73; Beverly's story, 47–48; Edna's story, 78, 79, 80, 81, 83–84; Ella's story, 29–30; guiding questions for, 108–109; Julia's story, 38, 41; Sarah's story, 55–56, 57
Reading at school: Angel's story, 68–71, 69, 73; Beverly's story, 51–52; Edna's story, 77, 80, 82, 83, 84, 86; Ella's story, 34–35, 35–36; guiding questions for, 110–111; Julia's story, 39–40; Sarah's story, 56–57, 60–61

RECOLLECTIONS, 25–86; Angel's story, 64–74; Beverly's story, 44–54; Daphne Key's story, 9–14; Edna's story, 74–86; Ella's story, 27–37; implications from, 88–92; Julia's story, 37–44; Sarah's story, 54–64

REDEFINITION, 31

RELIGION. *See* Performance at church; Reading at church; Writing at church

RESEARCH: guiding questions for evaluating, 114; implications from, 88–92

RESISTING SHUTDOWN, 101–103

S

SAFE HOUSES, 32

SARAH, 17, 23–24, 54–64

SCHOLAR/TEACHERS, 18

SCHOOL: as house of language-on-its-own, 5, 40. *See also* Performance at school; Reading at school; Writing at school

SELF-ESTEEM, 39

SHUT OUT, 89–90

SHUTDOWN, 3–4, 92–96; absolute, 91; Angel's story, 64–74; Beverly's story, 44–54; Daphne Key's story, 9–14; Edna's story, 74–86; Ella's story, 27–37; families and, 90–91; Julia's story, 37–44; memory of, 89–90; process of, 89; questions raised by, 88; resisting, 101–103; Sarah's story, 54–64

SHUTTING PEOPLE OUT, 96–101

SILENCE, 5–6, 13; definition of, 5

SKILLS, 102

"SOMEBODY'S MOTHER", 71

SOUTHERN LIVING, 41

STUDENTS: ABE, 6, 93; redefinition of, 12, 13; vocational, 12

T

TEACHERS, 36, 99; English, 18, 24, 73; of literacy, 79; perceptions of, 90; scholar/teachers, 18

TEACHING READING: Angel's story, 67; Beverly's story, 52–53

TEACHING WRITING: Edna's story, 81, 82

TEN BOOM, CORRIE, 48

TERMINOLOGY, 42, 44

TIME, 47

TO KILL A MOCKINGBIRD, 35

V–W

VOCATIONAL STUDENTS, 12

WAITING TO EXHALE (MCMILLAN), 72